CW00853995

NEIL TAYLOR is a coach and behavioural skills change trainer with twenty-five years' experience in the development of people. As a lawyer and management consultant he passionately believes each person is the designer of their life, with accountability for the way they live it. Neil lives in Canary Wharf, London.

Clues from the Universe

Designing Your Life

Clues from the Universe
Designing Your Life

Neil Taylor

ATHENA PRESS
LONDON

CLUES FROM THE UNIVERSE
Designing Your Life
Copyright © Neil Taylor 2008

ISBN: 978 1 84748 321 8

First published 2008 by
ATHENA PRESS
Queen's House, 2 Holly Road
Twickenham TW1 4EG
United Kingdom

Printed for Athena Press

You absolutely sure you're ready for this?

It all starts here…

For Saz

Contents

'Walk towards the edge,' he said.
'We're afraid,' they said.
'Walk towards the edge,' he said.
'We're afraid,' he said.
'Walk towards the edge,' he said.
They walked towards the edge,
he pushed them
and they flew.

Guillaume Apollinaire

The Beginning

'*What if you woke up one morning and everything you thought you knew had changed?*'

'How do you mean?'

'*Well, what if the universe had flipped upside down, or just plain turned inside out. Use your imagination: at traffic lights people feel anxious on blue, squirrels are now in charge, that type of thing. How would it feel?*'

'Weird, I suppose. *Very* weird. Squirrels, eh? How would I know what to do? How would I know if what I was doing was OK?'

'*How do you know now?*'

'You just do, don't you? It's in the rules. We've all been doing it for so long that it's just what you … do.'

'*Do you?*'

'Of course. You can't not do. That wouldn't be done. We all do, it's what we spend our lives… doing.'

'*OK, OK. Well, what if you woke up one morning and not doing was the new doing. The rules you talk about have all changed.*'

'You mean, like right was wrong and black was white, there was suddenly a reason for self-serving point scoring, that type of thing?'

'*No.*'

'No?'

'*No. Use your imagination here. What if there was no "right". It is just not recognisable as an option. What if "right" was off the scene? It's not that it doesn't matter anymore what is "right", it's that it is a non-issue.*'

'But you can't not have a right. There has always been a right. It is what helps us to feel good when we do it, enables us to get others to feel bad when they don't do our version of it, and gives everyone else something to aim at, look forward to, talk about in Starbucks.'

'*Who started it, this "right"?*'

'Hell, I don't know; Jesus, Muhammad, some woman in a cave, Ramses II, Walt Disney. Does it matter?'

'What if they got it wrong, these people? What if they happened to decide all this stuff on a morning when they woke up and the universe had changed, but they didn't know it? What if they were only kidding, or thought they were only deciding for themselves and not for you? Would that make a difference?'

'It might. But it has pretty much stuck now, hasn't it? I mean, the squirrels wouldn't like it if we started to mess with "right" and "wrong". And you'd have a heck of a job getting it past the lawyers. I mean, "How do you plead?" "I cannot possibly say with any certainty, ask me another." You couldn't found a multi-hierarchical, precedent-based legal system on that, could you?

'There would be mayhem, looting in Tesco; people would randomly drown expendable relatives. It wouldn't work.'

'What if "working" wasn't an issue anymore, and whether or not it "worked" didn't matter?'

'You know all this is nonsense, don't you? Mankind has finally clawed itself up to an evolved state where some things are non-negotiable. Language and rules are there for a reason. What else would students talk about over toast at three in the morning? I mean, "Hey man, what are we all here for?" "We're not." It would kill them.

'This all sounds like a philosophical waste product. You cannot just reinvent the universe overnight and expect people to do what the squirrels say. There has always been right and work and happy and death. It's how we motivate ourselves; it keeps us all in our place.'

'What if the universe only changed for you? The others could keep their rules, luxuriate in "right" and "wrong", look forward to tomorrow and fear death the day after. But you, you wake up and everything you thought you knew had changed…'

'It wouldn't happen.'

'You woke up this morning, didn't you?'

'The universe hadn't changed.'

'How could you possibly know? You expect there would be some kind of celestial fanfare or an announcement on CNN just for you?'

'There were no clues lying around. The sky was still grey, everyone looked glum on the bus, the markets were timidly rallying after four consecutive days of something record-breakingly bad. It all seemed pretty much the same to me.'

'*And these are the kind of clues you think you get from the universe, are they? It is just this mediocre, maxed-out dull thing?*'

'No, not just that. It's also an arithmetically perfect explosion of matter and gases careering out from a centre of unimaginable size and power infinitely uncontained in a sea of the inexplicable.'

'*And that's what you think the universe is, do you?*'

'Try me on the alternative.'

'*What if the universe could be contained in your head?*'

'This is a spatial irony thing, right?'

'*If you like. What if when we talk about everything you know having changed it is actually a realisation that the universe is contained within your head?*'

'And that is the thing that has changed?'

'*Ironically, no. That has always been the same. It's your realisation of it that has changed. How would that feel?*'

'That would change things.'

'*What things?*'

'All things. Everything.'

'*How would that feel?*'

'Scary.'

'*You have the power of the universe exactly where you want it, all the control you could never dream of, and you are afraid?*'

'Terrified.'

'*What are you afraid of?*'

'Well, everything. What if, for example, an unfettered thought slunk into my mind about killing all of the puppies in the world?'

'*With ultimate power comes ultimate control. The puppies are safe.*'

'But what if I don't want all of this ultimate power and ultimate control?'

'*Maybe that is what has really changed on this morning that the universe is different. It is no longer about what you want or don't want, but who you are. You can learn to transcend your wants, in the same way as you can remember the ability to get along without the need for "right" or things that are regarded as "working".*'

'*If you had all of the power of the universe you would no longer need to want.*'

'I think I might miss it.'

*'What you think you would miss is being what you thought you were –
attached to the rules and habits of the generations that spawned you. You
hang on to them because you know them, not because you believe in them.'*

'I didn't think I had the choice.'

*'You have the choice to be a creator rather than an inheritor. The choice
to wake up one morning and decide that the universe has changed.
Simultaneously you then realise that all pre-existing rules and laws no
longer apply.'*

'Now I know why I am so terrified by this thought. There
would be mayhem! Everyone simultaneously making up new
rules, or worse, making up no rules at all. Bloody hell, the French
can't even manage queuing – and they had a civil war.'

*'This is just you. The universe is contained within your head. You have
the control as well as all the power. That has been established. If others
choose to live by the rules of their forefathers that is for them. You are the
designer.'*

'Whoa! Am I God here?'

*'Can you point somewhere to a place outside yourself where God is?
Can you draw a line in the sand and place God on one side of it?'*

'Are you telling me that I am God?'

'Are you telling me that you are sure that you are not?'

'The God I know is huge, omni-everything, limitless, all
things…'

*'And this limitless wonder-being draws a line outside your head and
cannot, or does not want to, go in?'*

'No, no. That's not it. It's too simple. Or too difficult. What
about other people's heads? Why are there lines beyond which
God doesn't go for them?'

'Their heads and their choices are a matter for them.'

'So, they can have limitless power and universal choice as well
as me? How much limitless power is there exactly?'

*'You are asking me to place a definitive maximum on limitlessness?
Even with your present chosen preoccupation with rules and laws that
seems a little bizarre.'*

'Ignoring all of these other limitless universes inside everyone
else's heads for a moment, are you saying that I have ultimate
power and choice and can do with it what I will?'

'Or won't.'

'Or won't.'

'How does that feel?'

'Scary.'

'It seems you have a decision to make.'

'That's it? I just have to make a decision? My decision is the switch? I turn it on and *kaboom*… limitlessness?'

'If you are standing by a small switch that turns on the largest engine ever constructed it would seem a little ironic to say that all of the power is contained in the switch.'

'So my decision is the switch?'

'If it was, what would you turn on by using it?'

'The engine to understand all of this.'

'So turn it on.'

'But the puppies are safe, yes?'

The Dream

To many people it looked like just another place to meet and drink. Some of these people were sitting around it with other people who were sitting with them. Some were attempting conversation, others were contemplating it as a clumsy alternative to the uneasy silence that gripped them in its socially inept fist.

Two people sat at the bar a little apart; one of them was not yet a poet. A few metres away from them, his foot resting on a tarnished chrome rail, sat a man. He sat with the peak of a baseball cap pulled low over his forehead, wondering what the little groups of people at tables were talking about. To be truthful, he felt a little isolated and apart from those around him.

A person in one of the groups attempting conversation glanced across at a man at the bar whose face was partially obscured by the shadow of his hat, and wished he could be as comfortably alone with his drink as this man clearly was. As an undercover officer, he had been intensively trained to pick up non-verbal signals as the heartbeat of communication, and was fascinated with what those around him unwittingly emitted.

The carpet that played up to the sticky floorboards where the bar met the rest of the room was frayed in places where punters had frequently dragged the legs of their stools, pushing back to go to the gents, or to simply go away.

Bombay Mix had replaced peanuts in bowls on the bar, the core of what the owner announced as the radical management rethink of 'a 21st-Century Global Bar Image' he had read about in an airline magazine. The regulars had initially viewed this change with suspicion but gradually relented, picking peanuts from the rest of the mix as they inadvertently disproved someone's theory on the evolution of choice.

The man who had framed this theory, and who was attempting to place pictures and substance in the middle of the frame, was pursuing the most recent in his latest philosophical line of

social truths. He planned a book, possibly more. To him humanity was a gorged, protruding vein ripe for dialysis. He loved to
probe the way his species connected with itself and the
environment it inhabited. He was attracted to the uneasy
relationship human beings had with the intelligence that
surrounded them, which they sniffed at and explored, before
running from it when it became too hard to understand, like
meerkats responding to the peeping of their sentry guard.

His latest theory postulated that the more similar choices a
person makes the more independently sentient the choices
themselves become. Eventually, the choices become separate
from the person making them, and they assemble themselves.
Human beings were then left to fish for words to describe such
events. Many opted for the word 'coincidence', propounding
theories around it, then having them disproved by others who
mapped such events as the 90% likelihood that at least two
American presidents should be born on the same day. Others
chose the word 'probability', making helpful statements in
support of their stance, such as the chances of an event occurring
must be between nought and one.

Both of these camps slapped their heads in disbelief at the
certifiable section of the population who were happy to forego
mathematics and statistical analysis in favour of magic. For them,
the mystical and unexplained were a fundamental part of the
mischief of the planet. Unbeknown to the conscious part of all of
these forehead scathers, when the 'magic camp' chippily smiled
along and wondered at the sorcery of life, huge plates of the
universe aligned alongside them, waiting to be joined by their
incredulous detractors.

This picture-painting theorist had once driven through the
town in which this bar opened its doors. For the last ten miles of
his journey, and spurred on by some less than subliminal radio
advertising, he had been thinking about drink. He wanted one.
He had been close to making the choice to stop that would have
gone some way towards unwittingly satisfying his nearly formu-
lated theory, when a blinding ray of sunlight momentarily stole
the signage of the bar from his sight. He had driven on.

Now, ten days later, some of the people in this bar sat at one of the tables and drank alcopops. One of them wondered what exactly it was he was drinking. A lawyer, clipped and measured in the expression of a life he had not yet begun to properly lead, he realised how utterly inappropriate it was to drink this in company. But he loved the sparkle of it on his tongue. It tasted like much more than a drink – more like an occasion. He wondered if this was the occasion he was supposed to be drinking it at.

A woman sitting with him at his table wondered if she was his friend and what meaning this word might have in his life. Well, at least, she considered, they must be more than two lawyers jostling for air as they hurtled towards the glass ceiling at the same firm. She had ordered a bottle of lager and was focusing her attention on whether its adhesive label could be picked from it if she could find a corner to peel. On her suffocatingly liturgical dark formal jacket she was wearing an ice blue brooch, almost exactly the colour of the memory of her mother's eyes.

She glanced across at her friend and thought it was unusual that a man in monk shoes from corporate finance should have ordered a Raspberry and Blueberry Blaster. She wondered if their orders had been mixed up, then remembered that she had ordered lager and didn't like the taste of chemically excited raspberries.

Distracted, she glanced around the bar and tried to make out the expression on the face of one of the men who appeared to be lone drinkers at the bar. He was also drinking lager. She thought he might be peeling the label from the bottle in his hand, but the shadow cast by a column holding up the jukebox made it too dark to make this out for sure.

She had been examining a part of her life for a long while now. The loss that had been too great for words had now formed itself into a stone ball and was lying in the centre of her chest. It seemed strange how seeing men, randomly dotted around a bar, reminded her of him. She still wondered how a man like her husband could so quickly become her ex. The death of their daughter had torn at them with razor claws. The ferocity of this attack on their marriage and their lives had been like a fifteen-minute storm of such intensity that afterwards, as she lay gasping for breath and surveying the destruction around her, she almost couldn't remember their fourteen years together.

She did recall snapshots of the chaos that followed, but saw them as if she were an observer, looking through photographs of someone else's life. She saw him being taken away after the funeral, then kept so heavily sedated that he started to cease to exist, not only in the present but in their memories. The visits became less frequent as she fought at the bulwark of her grief to look after their two surviving sons. From somewhere she remembered a degree of envy when she heard about his first suicide attempt. How typically selfish of him. That's it, she thought, leave the world and let everybody else clear up after you.

Finally, she heard he had dealt with it; moved on. There was no envy this time. She couldn't imagine this. She didn't want to move on, it was too important to feel what she did. No, she more than felt it, but when she had finally broken through the ice wall that had formed around her heart and talked about it to a friend she had heard herself describing it as a 'feeling'. That felt odd, that specious word. She was certain it was more than a feeling and baulked at her own mistreatment of the sensibilities that defined her. She was looking at this part of her life as if the label on it could be peeled and removed from it. But she was unsure how to locate the corner that should first be picked at.

For so long the darkness in her life did not allow her to start the peeling process. Maybe this long winter would end and bring more light. The skies and landscape were leaden and endless. There was that wretched course in April imploring her to 'Design Your Future Life'; that would be her new deadline. Damn Human Resources, with their platitudes and training needs analyses! Damn them for their lies about moving on! Her pain was not behaviour that could be designed out of her; and yet she agreed to attend the charade, if only to put a stop to the emails with a colon, an 'o' and two smiley brackets from a girl who worked there and sported far too many vowels at the end of her forename to maintain a shred of dignity.

At least in April there would be lighter mornings and time to work things out. She had to think of something else – *anything* else – if only for the boys who remained and who regarded her with hooded eyes over the chasm of breakfast on the mornings they couldn't avoid each other.

She looked back at the label on the bottle of lager in front of her; one of the corners looked like it could still be picked away if only she could summon up the will to start it off.

Resolute winter sunlight struggled to penetrate the far corners of the bar. Mostly it stayed outside and teased the puddles on the pavements, waiting for cars to turn the corner just up from the bar's car park in order to bounce off dashboards and into the drivers' startled eyes.

The sun illuminated dried white bullets of flattened chewing gum that spelt out a join-the-dot plea for thoughtful litter disposal to a world that had its attention elsewhere.

An emissary of sunshine made its way through a pair of one of the windows' dust-thickened red curtains and pounced on the south end of the bar. Here it lit some beer rings and dried pools of spilt drinks that evidenced the part-time cleaner's recently acquired lack of concentration.

The cleaner was concerned about her son. She had always wanted him to be happy. This had become the words in the stick of rock which, when snapped, revealed the legend of her life. It seemed that now he was nearly old enough to choose the source of this happiness, he had determined to look in a place it couldn't be found.

She was unhappy. Her son was too, or at least he would be. He couldn't see it, of course, but she could. She was his mother.

She had realised this by unlearning everything about her life her own mother had tried to impose on her. Her mother never had the faintest clue about anything that could have made the daughter happy. The daughter, now a mother herself, sometimes believed she had even chosen to be unhappy to spite the old cow. There was so much she would teach her son; she'd make him listen. He wouldn't end up doing the stuff that she had done. She only wanted to make him happy.

He wouldn't find that on his so-called 'travels', and least of all on that ridiculous boat. Happiness was found at college, meeting the kind of people who would later own, not work on, boats. It was about looking good and being smart in places she had seen in the windows of travel agencies that held her dreams hostage.

The door of the bar opened with a squeak familiar to those

who had heard it often before. The man at the bar in the cap looked up for just long enough to catch the shape of the person coming through it. He looked down again sharply and, out of habit, pulled down at the peak of his hat but left enough of his face showing to be recognisable to the person who was scouting the room for people to sit with.

The man in the cap had forgotten that his initials were emblazoned above the peak like an announcement, and was unaware that the act of pulling his visor down actually broadcast more clearly who he was.

The last few months had become a time of great change for him. His core belief that real ale was all that ran through the arteries of the world had been shaken by catching his first ride on an emotional express that propelled itself through his life, his head, his consciousness... his very being. A woman with magnificent breasts and a smile as wide as an East End car salesman had gathered him up, sat him on this train, and for a while they had watched the landscape of everything around him change, before he was dumped unceremoniously on a siding somewhere down the track.

Rather than return him forcibly to his previous existence, the awakening of a part of himself he had never known coaxed him into previously uncharted territory. What he imagined had been love for this woman had led him by the hand to the smorgasbord table of life. He didn't like everything he saw, set out on platters and dishes at a buffet he had never experienced before. Poetry and CDs of great love classics were like rollmop herrings: they would never be to his taste. However, he happily trawled the salad bar of literature, filling a plate, previously piled with online multiplayer fantasy games and fists of beer, with explorative sorties into Austen, Trollope and C S Lewis. These expeditions to the table had led to a spiritual unfolding. He devoured Coelho and Covey in the quest to answer questions he had never posed before.

In doing so he learnt that when the student is ready the teacher will appear, and came to the realisation that while pain was an inescapable part of life it wasn't necessarily something he had to run from. He still came to the bar he now sat in wearing the cap, his trademark, but latterly entered it a wiser man with different answers.

Back in the sun-streaked bar the scout at the door, his ginger hair gelled up like neon stalactites, caught the announcement on the wiser man's cap and joined him at the bar.

'Miserable, isn't it?' the ginger man said.

'Is it?'

'Have you ever known it more miserable?'

The man in the cap was beginning to realise that he had not, as he had thought, felt lonely before. He had merely been on his own. He glanced again across the bar and briefly caught the eye of the woman wearing an amazing blue brooch, momentarily frozen in time by a ray of sunshine as it diffused from a glass on the table at which she was sitting. For her part she caught sight only of the peak of his cap, hiding the look from the eye she might otherwise have exchanged. She turned to avoid eye contact with the miserable looking ginger-haired man who had joined him. She had known him before, of course, but always as an ally of her husband. It was strange to see him here in a new context, but she was determined not to let him see her. The paths of their lives would, in fact, be designed to cross again when they chanced upon each other in the antechamber of what appeared to be an ordinary suburban house four months later. A design they fashioned for themselves and each other.

'Have you?'

'Have I what?'

'Known it more miserable.' The ginger man was determined to have a conversation with a man he had only met casually twice before. He pushed home his advantage. This was a conversation he needed to have. He didn't care who he had it with; his prey at the bar was only one of the many victims he'd never had in mind.

The man in the cap looked around the bar in the place and at the time that was being hailed as the most miserable. As he did the rays of sunlight bounced around the room, creating prisms of light that disappeared almost before they arrived. They skipped off the optics and toyed with some bottles on shelves above.

One of the rays launched itself at the blue brooch of the woman whose eyes had not yet opened again to the light it could bring. Bullseyeing, it ricocheted off and landed in the ashtray on the table at which the brooch's owner sat, from where it then diffracted and became instantly invisible.

Motes of dust crowded around to watch the sun at play. They were always ahead of the game, jostling as they waited in thermals and crosswinds for the rays to arrive, charging against each other to steal a better view.

When he looked at where the sun was the man in the cap couldn't imagine a more beautiful place.

'Doesn't it get on your tits?' the ginger man persisted, sensing his audience hadn't yet got in step with his thinking.

Startled by the intervention of this voice in his beautiful place, the cap lifted to look at his enquirer's face. 'Who does?'

'Who? No. *Everything*. Not just people. Who? Jeez, don't get me started!'

The man in the cap looked across to the ashtray for the remains of the sun. No sign. The rays were now playing in the doorway of a shop down the road.

'Do you want to know what I think?'

No, thought the cap. 'Yes,' he said.

'I think it's all going tits up.'

There was definitely a theme developing here. The imagery being used by his miserable companion was either unimaginatively limited or deliberately consistent. The man in the cap pulled firmly on its brim, but it had already reached its lowest level across his forehead.

'Do you want to buy me a beer?' asked the miserable man.

Absolutely not, thought the cap. 'OK,' he said.

A beer was bought. The bottle it came in was cold and wet. Its label looked like it would not even need picking; that it could slide right off the bottle. The woman with the blue brooch never even noticed; she had been distracted by something her monk-shoed colleague had said that was neither interesting nor amusing. In many ways this was a shame. It could have been the clue she was searching for, but she couldn't let the ginger-haired man see her. She couldn't bear to hear what he might have to say.

'It's a double rollover tonight.'

'Is it?'

'Yeah.'

The miserable man looked around the bar. He looked straight through the woman with the brooch. People seemed to be getting on with their lives despite the fact that opportunity was waiting down the road in the shop with the Lotto machine. He was unaware that the very ray of sun that had sported with the optic less than a metre away from where he sat had moved down to the Lotto shop's doorway an instant later. He touched the outline of the piece of paper in his pocket, feeling its crispness.

'Double rollover, about 20 million.'

Even if the man in the cap had been listening he still wouldn't have comprehended this. A thousand miles away, a trillion, it was just noughts to him. Eight grand to buy a thing he didn't need, or a lifetime of saving; he didn't want it. His smorgasbord offered him the temptation of many dishes but, for him, none tasted better on a bed of banknotes.

Instead he was thinking about how amazing it was to be hearing the murmur of other people's conversations while watching the perfection of bubbles rising in advancing strings against the inside surface of his glass. Despite his miserable drinking companion (or more likely because of what his presence made him realise) he had settled into the wonder of this moment of being alive.

The miserable man, his white arms sporting a coat of pale auburn hairs, checked his pocket again. The Lotto ticket was still there. He jabbed at the arm of the man on the other stool.

'What could I do with 20 million?'

The man in the cap made a noise that simulated both attention and response. It was the audible equivalent of a waved hand gesture suggesting his companion should continue. 200,000 years of the evolution of language, accelerated in the last ten by sitting in front of computer screens and ignoring everyone around, had not been wasted. This kind of gesture said, 'OK, I'm part of this conversation at a very peripheral level and will dip in and out of it as required, so get on with it.' It worked.

'I'll tell you what. Everything, that's bloody what.'

The miserable ginger man looked at the cap for any indication that he might continue. This could hardly be regarded as a polite pause, but it served as such. It was at this moment that his chosen

prey, a man who had recently placed mizuna salad ic.
solettes with cep sauce on his plate of life, realised that he u.
want something from this conversation. It came as much of a
surprise to him as it would have done to anyone observing the
interchange between them so far. The person in the bar who
might have been most interested had taken a last determined swig
of lager from her glass and was preparing to return to work for the
afternoon. She put the jacket with the blue brooch over her
shoulders, slightly masking her face, and followed the monk
shoes out of the bar.

In his mind's eye the man in the cap looked at the miserable
man, imagined him with 20 million pounds in his hand and could
not see any difference. He just saw a miserable man struggling to
come to terms with the fact that his supposed dream win had not
given him everything he wanted. If anything he saw more misery,
it was just that his ginger-haired drinking companion would
indulge it in more salubrious surroundings.

'What can you do with 20 million pounds that you cannot do
with your life as it is?' The man in the cap tried one of a range of
questions his new, recently bruised life now came equipped with.

The miserable man looked at his inquisitor. With this question
their singularly one-dimensional relationship had been totally
recalibrated. Subconsciously he could never recall ever having
been asked any kind of question by the man on the other stool on
the two occasions they had sat at this very bar. On a conscious
level he thought he must be a complete knob.

'*What?*' he asked, although the question was clearly redundant.
In a single word he described the length and breadth of the knob
he thought the man in the cap to be. However, his companion
decided to take this as the question it was clearly not intended to
be.

'What makes you think your life would be any different if you
had 20 million pounds?' The question was so similar to his
previous one as to hardly invite a different answer. He was yet to
perfect his new technique.

'*What?*' The ginger man, miserable to the core, did not dis-
appoint the natural geometry of the conversation.

The circle of question and answer closed at that point. It had the potential to go round and round at this stage but make no progress. It needed an intervention.

'Are you are complete knob?' said the miserable man. And there it was, a new beginning to the conversation.

The man in the cap decided that he could not answer this question. He also realised there was no need for an answer. There was no time for it in any event.

'You're mad. Bonkers! 20 million quid, no difference? What's *wrong* with you?'

The ginger-haired man had erected fortified barriers many years ago. This was the way he dealt with a life that had for so long seemed out of control. He was so self-unaware that he would have been shocked to hear how he held his breath when returning home from work each night, wondering if his wife would still be there.

Their lives had become a habit; she was his and he was hers. As she told him about her day, he thought about food and the time the game was due to start on TV. Their lovemaking had become routine and a testament to her powers of visualisation. She once raised the possibility of couples therapy, but he only heard the voice of his boss at a recent appraisal criticising his powers of listening. He barked at her that if she wanted couples therapy she would have to go alone, and that night she dreamed of a man on a boat sailing her away into the sunshine. Away from a man who had become victim of his daily commute and the pointless sales meetings it led him to and from.

But despite all of the damage the last few years had bestowed on his confidence he knew stupidity when he heard it. How could this idiot think such a thing? 20 million quid would make him rich. It would make him feel everything he couldn't feel now he wasn't rich. That ludicrous cap was obviously squeezing the sense out of the brain of a man he hardly knew. He half expected to see it emerging from out of his ears.

The capped man tried a question from his new, enlightened winter collection. 'But what if you discovered you were rich and miserable?'

'How could that happen? How could I ever be miserable? Didn't you hear me – it is 20 million quid!' The miserable man who needed this huge sum of money to buy himself a new description thought that, perhaps, this crazy cap man had misheard him. Perhaps he thought he said twenty quid.

'What would be different in your life?' The man in the cap got to his point. At some level he thought that asking the question differently would enable them both to understand.

'You want me to make a list?'

In a perfect world this is the stage the conversation would have ended for the man in the cap. He did not, in fact, want a list. He had a pretty good idea what would be on it. He was now extremely unclear as to why he had asked any questions at all of this person for whom misery had been momentarily replaced by rancour. Even the bubbles in his glass seemed to have stopped their upward progress. The universe seemed less perfect, and he had a horrible realisation he was about to be sucked into the wretched world of this hapless human being.

Anger and desperation raised a big, ginger-knuckled hand and started ticking off points.

'I would be rich.' That took at least two fingers, the second one for emphasis. 'I would take a First Class flight to the Caribbean where I would hire myself a fuck-off yacht.' Two more ticked off. 'I would lie around rich in the sun for a month, looking rich. And, er...'

He had reached his thumb and clearly felt that he was about to make his most important point.

'And my missus would be there. It's not been good with her for a while, but I would be rich, on a boat, in the Caribbean and that would be it. *Kaboom!* Everything sorted, and I would see her smile again. Because she would be rich, too.'

The man in the cap looked at the miserable man. It was clear he really believed that, free with every Lotto win, came a life that was magical and healed. There was an odd moment of silence between the two of them. The miserable man looked straight into the eyes beneath the cap and appeared to be silently calling for his drinking companion to agree with him. Gone was the bravado of the £20 million winner. This was a dream more fragile than it had appeared when it walked into the bar with him. In fact, it was more than a dream; it was something he needed, depended upon, took out and showed himself at times when other people were not around.

He had taken it out in this gloomy bar and flashed it before this man in a cap who he barely knew.

His bar stool companion saw all of this in the look they were exchanging. To him it was incredible that this miserable man had constructed such an important part of his life around six numbers on a ticket that could result, despite the statistically huge improbability etched in the odds against, in a very large number.

In this strange moment, as their gaze held, the miserable man reached automatically into his pocket and felt for the piece of paper. He squeezed it between his thumb and forefinger.

'That sounds great,' said the man in the cap. Not a single part of him believed it.

'Do you think any of these people recognise us from the papers?'

He still couldn't quite work out which of the huge array of buttons on the console at his right hand worked the seat into a bed. There were more of them lined up than on his mate's remote control, and he had more audio-visual equipment than anyone else down the road.

His wife was not concentrating on the question. She was trying to work out where she was going to put the magazines she had taken from the lounge. The pocket in the seat in front of hers was about twenty feet away and once she was strapped in (which she intended to be for the entire flight) how would she get to it?

'I'm sure that a couple of passengers who walked past us a minute ago on their way down to Economy gave me a look,' he persisted. Celebrity was as new to him as the shirt on his back and he wore them both with a mixture of pride and discomfort.

'They probably spotted the nine packets of biscuits sticking out of your jacket pocket,' she said. 'You're not supposed to take those out of the lounge, you know.'

Sure, he thought, well they would get really goggle-eyed over the glass etched with 'Premier Class' he'd stuck in his hand luggage as they had left to walk to their gate. He'd had half an eye on the bottle of Jim Beam, but couldn't work out how to seal the lid on so it wouldn't spill out into his new brown bag with fussy motifs like the ones the rich carry as a flag of their wealth all over the world.

'They're part of the whole First Class experience,' he tried.

'Well, so are the glasses and cutlery, but you didn't have it away with them, did you?' She was getting tetchy. She didn't like flying, and the thought of eight hours with her husband in his ridiculous orange shirt and an electric chair was not making the pain behind her eyes any better. She regretted the second Dubonnet, now. She'd never tried it before, and the second glass tasted more hideous than the first.

She told the stewardess that she was quite comfortable and would keep her coat with her. The air conditioning was blowing on her knees and she wasn't absolutely sure she had taken the price tag out of the coat when buying it in a rush the day before yesterday. Also, she didn't know how the air conditioning nozzle worked and wondered if it would affect the engines if she started playing with it.

She didn't want to accept the champagne, but thought she better had. Two other passengers across the cabin had theirs and, observing them, she could now see where to rest the glass. No one published a list of rules about the etiquette of travelling First Class for the first time, and she wasn't sure how much stuff she could order on the tickets they had bought.

In the next seat, her husband had said 'yes' to the warm nuts in a little china bowl that must have been made to do nothing but hold warm nuts. She wondered if they now had to buy some of those little china bowls to put nuts in when people came round. Where would you get them from? Could you put them in the microwave? How long would it take to warm nuts in them? She was sure she had never seen any instructions about warming on any packet of nuts she had ever bought. It was amazing the new things you had to pay attention to when you suddenly became rich.

'What's this?' said her husband irritatingly, holding out a macadamia nut.

'It's a hazelnut,' she said, 'it's fine. Just eat it.'

'Tastes funny.'

'Well, leave it then.'

'I might keep this,' he said holding up the little china bowl. 'It would be good for my maggots.'

She looked at him. He was such a moron. Her sister had said he would look much more attractive now they had money. So far he just managed to look like a rich moron.

'Do you think they give a different safety demonstration in First Class?' he asked, flicking through the 'What's On Up Here?' pages of the in-flight magazine, skipping an article on the '21st-Century Global Bar Image'.

She hardly heard. She was calculating that if she now asked for a bowl of nuts and they had them again on the return flight, they could steal the four nut bowls and that would save looking for them when they got back. She was pretty sure four nut bowls would do it.

'I mean, do you think our life jackets are under our seats, or will they come round with them on a tray?'

Ignoring him, she looked at her bag which was safely stowed under the seat in front of her about forty yards away. What were the rules, for example, on knitting in the First Class cabin?

'You'll never get those needles past customs,' her husband had told her in the limousine on the way to the airport. It was a bit late to tell her then. She had fretted as they unloaded their luggage and felt like a criminal during baggage check-in. Her husband delighted in pointing to the signs all over the airport about the items banned from hand baggage, and she was almost sick at the check-in desk as they asked her, in velveteen voices, about who had packed her bags and what she had allowed to be placed in them. Even at this stage she felt that she couldn't raise the issue of a few knitting needles with these nice people, who were focused upon the wafting and cosseting of premier air travel. They were so nice, and she was First Class. Probably the rules were different for people like them and their money anyway.

But she needn't have worried. Her bag glided through all the X-ray checks at Heathrow, the security staff being much more concerned about people with too many coins in their pockets and overlarge belt buckles that set off their sophisticated machines than a few innocent knitting needles.

She would think about it later. As she looked out of the window she missed her husband sneaking a glance at her. He was still hoping to see her smile. Surely this trip would do it. He hadn't seen her smile in ages. But she was rich now; that had to make a difference.

He braved the opening of half an eye. The dream looked different when illuminated by the slatted light of the afternoon sun as it poured through the blind-covered porthole and into the main guest stateroom.

He moaned, even though there was no one within yards to hear him. Twenty-four hours of sleep had done little to ease his suffering. The hop from Antigua had probably been the worst part. The plane had bumped and skewed through tiny rain clouds, but his concentration had been on a wax-coated paper bag five inches from his face. He had missed the island's impressive volcanic outline, blurred by palm, mango and breadfruit trees as the tiny single-engined propeller plane hung low, seeking out the landing strip on the final part of his journey from hell into hell.

He was vaguely aware of his wife pointing out white timber-framed plantation cottages being consumed by hibiscus and other vividly edged tropical foliage as he emptily retched into the bag one more time. He had imagined this triumphant arrival onto Nevis so many times since the moment the unimaginable win had been finally confirmed by a Lotto executive who he believed had been more excited by the event than he was.

Now his back ached from the heaving that had started two hours before Antigua. His head screamed in pain but was still capable of registering the twisting ache in his stomach which joined in an anguished waltz with the throes of his limbs.

He didn't care about the swinging vervet monkeys or parts of steaming local lobsters being described by their jeep driver, who clearly did not have a change of script for 'arrival of sick yacht hirer'. He just wanted to kill his wife, grab the wheel and end all of their suffering at once. How could an island that was only six miles across have so many roads? And why were there more goats than tarmac on all of them?

He barely remembered arriving at the yacht. One of the five great moments of his life, and he was wondering if he could make it to the head in time! He didn't, and it became, as he believed at this instant, one of the five worst.

The crew were polite and helpful, but bemused. His wife disappeared, exhausted from clucking around a man she had stopped caring for far earlier than two hours before Antigua. If this was to be one of the top five greatest moments in her life she was going to enjoy every spangled second of it. The *Vita Da Sogno* was more beautiful than its pictures in the brochures. Its pure white lines seemed to stretch across the water, entirely unbroken. Where shadows etched their furrows they only accentuated the places where sunlight described the curve of the two of its four decks she could see from the quayside. Floor to ceiling glass wrapped around the main saloon creating a fishbowl view of the deck, sea and endless vistas this magic carpet of a boat could whisk people to.

She had no idea where 'aft' was, but she sure as hell was going there to be pampered. Hell, at twenty-five grand a week she was going to redefine the word 'pamper' and make it into the verb of the year.

Meanwhile her husband was led down a whirling staircase by the marginally least bemused member of the crew to a cherry-wood room lined in parquet and white leather, where he too disappeared for the next day.

He closed the half opened eye as the door swung open.

'How are you feeling?'

For him at that moment the boat lurched violently, sending a stabbing pain through his fevered head. The motion caused flashes of painful light to streak across his inner vision. For her there was a gentle ripple as 120 feet of hull brushed gently against the swell stirred by a passing fishing boat. It was a motion that had thrilled her all night as she sat on deck watching shooting stars chasing each other across the constellations. In that time she became at rest with herself. She smiled inwardly; if this was jet lag, she wanted more of it in more exotic locations.

He heard the question but did not think he could answer. Adjectives tumbled around his brain but none of them clung to a noun.

'Do you think it was the seafood?'

He didn't think at all. Thinking was too painful.

'Seafood on board a plane can't be good for you.' She knew this wasn't a propitious line of conversation, but couldn't help it. There was no reaction from her husband. She wasn't sure she wanted one.

He rolled over in bed, taking the sheets with him. She noticed briefly (and, she thought, oddly) that the white of his belly, brushed with a faint ginger down, matched the parchment-coloured cotton sheets. No, she *did* want a reaction.

'Serves you right,' she wanted to say. 'Serves you right for pigging yourself out on the plane and embarrassing me. Serves you right for that stupid shirt, those stupid trousers and those stupid, stupid trainers that you bought to travel in to the Caribbean to catch my dream boat. Serves you right for ignoring me for the last nine years. Serves you right for all those nights spent down the bar. Serves you right for all those nights you could have been down the bar but stayed at home and were miserable with me. Serves you right for making me miserable when I could have been happy and out there and just, just...'

'Serves you right,' she said and stormed out.

He rolled over again and opened half an eye to watch the door closing behind her.

'You have to eat something.' She had just finished the most amazing lunch of pan-seared mahimahi diced with lemon grass, ginger and tamarind. 'Jean-Pierre can do incredible things with food.'

He propped himself up on three or four pillows. The room went hazy and he turned towards the view out of his port hole. It framed the usual vista: an aluminium railing and part of an orange circle that he couldn't quite place as an object. It had become his world for three days.

'I don't want food. I don't want anything.' This was the first sentence he had constructed in all of his time on board the yacht. When he woke up on the first day he had hoped to feel better. On the second day he had forgotten what it was like to feel anything but awful. On the third day he wished he felt like he had on the first day.

'The doctor says that if you don't eat something you could die.' She meant to appear sympathetic when she said this. Her reflection had looked quite sympathetic when she had rehearsed it earlier in a mirror in her cabin, preparing for this conversation. But she couldn't quite carry it off live in front of a man whose funeral, over the years, she had repeatedly planned down to the last detail.

The doctor had been called in yesterday. He came highly recommended by the Four Seasons Resort on Pinney's Beach and certainly looked the part. His bedside manner was invested in the creases of his trousers and shirtsleeves. He had fumbled around for a while, tapping various bits of her husband's repulsive, miserable white body and sighing before administering an injection guaranteed to make him feel better.

He returned in the middle of the night when the first signs of an adverse reaction to the injection set in. He examined his patient and tutted a great deal, in a way he'd seen in a medical soap opera on television. This was the first time transfer to the hospital in Charlestown was mooted. The doctor seemed very doubtful that this would be a good idea. People attending the hospital were inclined to feel much better on the journey there.

There were a few health clinics on Nevis but these were much better utilised for those who were generally healthy or who had been involved in a diving incident.

'Will your husband want a hyperbaric chamber, do you think?' he asked dubiously.

'Do you think he needs one? What is it for?' she had asked.

'Well, if he has the bends this is the best way. But we do not have such a chamber on the island,' he added pleasantly, 'so maybe we should leave it.'

'OK,' she said. Thinking, Let's keep our options open here; you almost certainly cannot hear him whinging in a decompression chamber.

'Remind me, has he been diving? It may be the bends.'

'He doesn't have the bends, he has the squits,' she said. 'Can't you inject him again?'

The doctor had looked at the ashen face of this gloomy white man lying in what, to him, was an amazing stateroom on board this ship of dreams. His features had taken on the quality of pale oily fish skin. He told the woman it was unwise to inject him again; the cure appeared to be making him worse.

'Oh, go on,' she said.

'He could die... and he must eat. It is important that he eats. You have a chef, yes?'

Now standing in the bedroom of the yacht with her back to the Caribbean she remembered this conversation and reminded the patient of it. 'You must eat. What can I get Jean-Pierre to make for you? Bloody hell, we have a cordon bleu chef on board who is employing several stars and a vicious French temper making me snacks. He must be able to whip up something for you. What about a steak? Toast? A bowl of Coco Pops?'

'Go away,' he said.

She needed no further encouragement. She went away.

Four days later the doctor was just leaving at the end of his daily visit. He no longer felt it right to suggest a move to the hospital. He looked around the *Vita Da Sogno*. Merely recommending a transfer to their drab little island didn't seem expensive enough somehow. He thought it would be much more dramatic to airlift him to St Kitts, then on to the States. His father, the doctor, always said to him that seven days into a sickness is a week closer to death.

The sick man's wife had befriended this doctor and asked him more about his life on the island before he lowered himself into the motor launch that would carry him back to the beach.

'You should see it, it is beautiful here.'

'Yes,' she said, 'if only I could.' She abstractedly averted her gaze towards the part of the boat where her husband was lying in a state. The doctor mistook this glance for the enquiry that she had so far omitted to make during this latest of their many conversations.

'He is a little better. Drinking water now.'

'Oh,' she said absently. 'Good.'

The doctor looked at her again. 'Why are you here? On this yacht?'

She looked now towards the shore and at the soft white sand of Oualie Beach that edged gingerly up against the fringes of the rainforest. She had spent hours sitting on the top deck of the *Vita Da Sogno* watching pelicans diving for fish, seemingly oblivious of brown-skinned dreadlocked men in slashes of coloured cloth mending their nets and casting them experimentally into the surf. The occasional jet ski cut through this field of blue carrying youngsters, wrapped in concentration and splashed by self-fashioned wakes, exploring the magical coves of what she had come to think of as her part of the island.

From this vantage point she could see the rising shores of St Kitts and beyond that, no doubt, the Dominican Republic and on past Haiti and Cuba to mainland America. Why was she here?

'We won the Lotto about a month ago, me and him.' She waved her arm towards what she now knew to be aft. 'It's a game people play, with paper and numbers.'

The doctor looked at her and creased his brow. She had come to recognise this as his way of dealing with those parts of the English language that had no place in the vocabulary of his world.

'This boat is part of his dream. A dream he always talked about; the First Class flight, the yacht, the Caribbean...' she tailed off and looked again across to the beach.

'Is it your dream too?' He was now sitting in the bobbing motor launch. The crew member sitting by the outboard motor was idly playing with some foam lying on the waves.

'How could it not be? I mean, look at it.' She looked around at the freshly washed decks of the *Vita Da Sogno*. Two crew members were polishing the chrome on an already perfectly shiny railing just above them. They were immaculate in their pressed white uniforms.

All around them the soft lines of the boat merged into glass abutted by teak decking. From the sun pads to the main decks, and reflected back from the long tinted windows like eyes winking at the ocean, it appeared that someone had once sketched some free-flow thoughts onto a piece of paper and given them to a boat builder to join together. The result was this wonderfully imagined craft.

She looked again at the doctor.

'I think my dream is out there somewhere.' She scanned the shore as she spoke, waving her arm this time away from the boat.

The doctor smiled. He was not sure he was supposed to understand.

He said, 'So, he is living this dream in there, is he?'

She smiled too. 'Ironic, isn't it?' she said. The doctor looked at her and creased his brow. In fact, he understood fully.

After the doctor left she felt an unusual pang of guilt. She had no idea where it had come from, but it led her into her husband's room. He looked up from his nest of pillows as she entered the cabin. She stood in the doorway for a few seconds, looking at this frail little rich man with big hands and small conversation.

'Ironic, isn't it?' she said, but not enough to herself.

'What?'

'Nothing. Look, you have to eat something. Is there anything at all I can get Jean-Pierre to cook for you?'

This conversation had become a staple with them. She would ask, he would refuse, she would fuss with the jug holding his drinking water for a few seconds and go away again. Twice she had stayed for a while and read magazines sitting on a sofa at the foot of the bed, but this only prolonged the agony.

'Maybe some soup.'

'What?' she snorted. The pattern had changed. Somewhere out in the universe, startled protons collided with some neutrons and then instantaneously realigned.

'Some soup,' he repeated.

'What sort of soup? I am sure Jean-Pierre can...'

'Heinz tomato soup. Not the foreign kind, either.'

'You can't ask a cordon bleu chef to make you Heinz tomato soup.'

'He doesn't need to, Heinz make it.'

'We're in Nevis, not Telford,' she said. 'Where is he supposed to get Heinz soup in the Caribbean?'

'From a shop,' he replied.

Now he said it she realised there may be some sense to it. It was typical, though. She would have to ask a crew member to go to Charlestown, or somewhere, and fetch some bloody English soup.

'You get it,' he said.

'What?' She could not believe him. He would send her traipsing around the island for soup.

'Why don't you get it for me? You haven't been off the boat yet and it will do you good.'

'I don't want to be done good to, thank you.' But even as she said it she wondered why she had not yet left the yacht. It was not through lack of invitation or opportunity. Several times the crew had suggested a trip onto the island. Moving the boat was out of the question, what with the misery's illness and access to the doctor, but she had resisted any trip ashore. Why?

'Do you want anything else while I am down there? Maybe some thick sliced white and brown sauce?'

He was too tired to do this. His weariness came not just from seven days of fasting and vomiting, but nine years of bickering. He turned his head, apparently once more towards the aluminium railing and part of an orange circle, but in fact just away from his wife. She hesitated for another couple of seconds and left the cabin.

'*Soup!*' she cried out theatrically, as she walked up the stairs to the main saloon, onto the aft deck and towards the launch that had now returned from the doctor's trip to the shore.

'I need soup,' she said to the crew member who helped her settle into one of the seats. She adjusted her sunglasses over her eyes as they pushed away from the yacht.

'Yes, madam,' he replied.

Together they headed down the island for Charlestown. She trailed her fingers in the water as they went and watched the magic bubbles dance around them from the silver of the surf.

In nearly every way, the Best Buy Supermarket was exactly what she was not expecting. In place of the imagined rolls of dust-covered coloured cloths there was a deep freeze full of low fat pasta meals.

Where she had expected open sacks of dried beans and lentils she found herself looking at clean white shelves of internationally recognisable labels, some of them exhorting her, exactly as they did at home, to lose weight by only adding them to her calorie controlled diet. Even Paul Newman smiled back at her and advised her to eat his sauce with the same expression as he did at home.

Substituting for quirky local gifts made of shell and tobacco twine was a selection of DVDs to rent, including three movies she had promised herself she would see at home just before the whirlwind of the win had cast them towards the Caribbean.

Rather than the dearth of Heinz soup she had predicted, there was a battalion of more than 57 flavours led from the front by the same classic tomato as she had in her kitchen cupboard.

And instead of the leering, intrusive and unsettling locals she had imagined scuttling around her as she foraged through her purse for mystifying foreign currency, there was a man moulded by the hands of the gods handing her a ten East Caribbean dollar note.

'Please take it,' this god said. He had waited patiently in the queue forming behind her as she battled with the contents of her handbag.

She threw him what she hoped was a smile that said, 'Actually no, but don't be offended and, hang on, why?' Frantically, she searched harder. The crew member who had brought her here in a jeep was now hanging out in the car park with five or six locals and could not be diverted from his conversation by her frenzied little waves as she widened the search to take in the pocket of her skirt.

'Please, he said, 'it's worth about two quid. You can owe me.'

'You're English?' she said.

There it was again, that smile. It creased the skin beside his eyes in a way that evidenced the fact that he had smiled that way many times before.

'Scottish,' he said. Scottish and six feet something, forty-ish, gently bearded and dazzling as a bank of halogens. He was standing beside her at the check-out framed on one side by a slice of perfect Caribbean blue sky and on the other by root vegetables.

'I couldn't.' She could, but wouldn't.

'Why not?'

'It's the rules,' she said. She leant a little closer to him as if to share the global conspiracy. 'Didn't you know?'

'The rules?' That smile again. 'You know you miss so much when you've been away from the rule-makers for as long as I have.'

'You live on the island?'

'Six years now. The first three years as a bum, the last three as a boat builder. I have my own business on the other side of the island. Near Indian Castle Beach. It's a time warp here, but that only matters if you care about time.'

Exasperated by the fruitlessness of her search for change, she decided that she could after all. She did, paid and they made their way towards the exit. She didn't know now, and would only find out much later, that he had first spotted her across one aisle of Best Buy as she was peering at the soups. He would have missed her, but he really fancied soup that day. He hadn't wanted soup for about six years.

He watched her put two cans of tomato in her basket. *Heinz*! He didn't even know that they sold Heinz soups in Best Buys. She looked even better in the glow of the check-out. She looked better still, a little flustered but glorious in her wrap-around bleached linen skirt and white T-shirt, as they stood together at the exit door.

'You have a car?'

'A jeep,' she said, 'it's not mine. It's part of the... do you drive here?' She thought about the state of the roads on the island and then looked around the car park to see if she could spot the car this man would drive.

'Bike,' he said.

'Motor or push?'

His laugh was the music to the score of his face. 'Motor.'

He loved the way she wrinkled her nose and then caught her sunglasses as they bounced precariously down it. He decided that he wanted to ask her to join him for a drink. He had forgotten the rules for this, too.

'Oh no,' she said, 'I really couldn't. I am on a mission.' It was out of the question.

They rode about two miles up the coast to Tequila Sheila's, a beachside café on Cades Bay. Her hair flew towards the sea and she found herself breathlessly pressed against his back as they ducked in between fallen vegetation, goats and somnambulant islanders who had no respect for the code of the road.

Over fresh mango juice from a shared jug he told her he had spent six years reinventing himself and learning that when he eventually found himself had discovered he wasn't him. When he finally decided not to worry about building a business and making a living it fell into place. He slowly became aware that he was a designer, not only of boats, but of his own life. This realisation was a major step on the journey that had taken him six years.

Thinking back later, he wondered if his recollection of it was the distortion of a romantically altered memory, but maybe it had been the special light of the morning as the sun rose over the view of his bay that day. Maybe he was complicit in his own internal mendacity and none of this had ever happened. Maybe there had been no decision before any of it had taken place. Maybe there had been no internal conversation.

It's just that, this morning, as he had chopped fruit and made coffee, he had never felt more like the designer of his life. He didn't have a plan, but followed his instinct and took the bike into town. He didn't know why, he hadn't been there for the longest time.

It was two hours after their drink at Cades Bay as they walked along his favourite beach at Newcastle on the Nisbet Plantation, a huge expanse of white sand shaded by coconut palms, that he heard for the first time about the recent good fortune she had shared with the husband he guessed she had. It was thirty seconds after that he dismissed it as irrelevant.

They used the same words at different times. Their language seemed to follow the same pattern, shaping and meeting in familiar formations. Although she knew she shouldn't, their fingers interwove, criss-crossing in a way that both of them recognised from a long way back. Somewhere in the universe more neutrons were busy skidding off orbiting electrons, creating the new constellations of the future.

'I have to go,' she said. 'I absolutely have to go.'

Four hours later they were sharing a main course of tannia fritters and grilled herb snapper at the Golden Rock Estate, being buzzed by evening hummingbirds and making wild decisions about green papaya pie. He could still hear her laugh over the local string band and she could still see him smile in the half-light.

That night she saw his boats for the first time. He talked to her about the way he fashioned wood to persuade it to curl into the shape he had imagined for it. She forgot to listen to the detail, part of her mind on a boat offshore. But she heard every word.

Three days later her husband received a note from her. It wasn't cruel, it asked for nothing. It wasn't wrapped around a tin of Heinz tomato soup. He was sitting for the first time on the aft deck of the *Vita Da Sogno*.

'It's from her.'

A crew member had been persuaded to sit with him. He wasn't uncomfortable about it, but he didn't know what he was expected to say. All of them had talked about this sick, miserable man's wife not returning to the boat. With only two guests it was hard not to miss one when she didn't come back from her shopping trip. Also, speculation travelled as fast as information on a small island in the Caribbean.

There had been word before, of course. A telephone call and a message carried by the doctor. Finally there was a note.

'She's not coming back.'

'Bummer,' said the crew member. As the only Englishman on the crew he was the natural choice for counsellor and confidant. He pulled his cap low over his forehead. The name of the *Vita Da Sogno* was emblazoned just above the peak.

'She's bunked off with a Scot.'

'Bummer.' He was doing well, despite having no formal training in trauma counselling. He was spending a year away from home and had found his way onto the yacht by a combination of pure fluke and a thirsty captain in a bar on Grenada. Pure fantasy, really, but what a job!

His mother, a cleaning lady who worked a number of bars back home, just didn't get it. She was always on at him to get a better life and proper education. How could university ever deal him a better hand than this? She just didn't, and never would, understand. He had never been happier in his life; just not right at this very moment, as his view of the ocean was blocked by the ginger haze of his rich, miserable man.

'I only wanted her to be happy.'

The young crew member thought to himself that she was

probably very happy right now, but decided not to pursue the point.

'Did you ever have a dream?' the miserable man asked of him.

'I'm only nineteen, I have lots of dreams.'

The miserable man looked at the crew member with the cap pulled down hard over his forehead. He realised that he could not see into his eyes.

'Do you know what my dream was?'

The nineteen years he had spent on the planet had not yet told this young man that some questions needn't be answered.

'No,' he said.

'My dream was to win the Lotto, fly First Class to the Caribbean, hire a fantastic yacht and share all that with my wife.'

The young man looked at him from under the peak of his cap. He was only nineteen, but old enough to realise that for the last ten days the other man had been living his dream. A dream he had probably religiously constructed over the years of not living it.

'That sounds great,' he said. Not a single part of him believed it.

The Clues

As he recalled, the box looked impossibly small. Obviously it could not sustain life, but surely it couldn't contain death either? He also remembered thinking that the plastic flowers which stood obliquely upright on its lid looked completely out of place. Their petals seemed, somehow, disproportionately large in relation to everything around them. Most of them looked as if they had been spray painted in colours that hurt his eyes. Some distant part of him was aware that it was an odd thing to think, in the same way that he knew they couldn't be plastic, but they weren't right. Nothing about this was right.

Someone tried to pull him away. The tug was gentle and well meant; someone who loved him felt he should be somewhere else.

'It's OK,' she said. All he saw was the blue flash of her eyes, reflected in the grossly large stone that clung to her jacket.

It's not, he thought. It's not. *It's not.* It's not! Nothing would ever be OK ever again. There were no words he could hear, nothing he could see, no place to go. He wanted to run but he could not leave her, alone in that box. Impossibly small.

He tried to look around but his eyes had forgotten how to focus. Nothing made any sense. He felt that he was no longer inside himself and that this emptiness was who he must be now.

It was then he remembered hearing the crying. It got louder and louder until it filled him. It wouldn't stop. It lasted for ten months.

When the crying was eventually over, it was as if the drugs they had given him had blocked the path between his brain and his tear ducts. He told them he was now fine, that he felt better. Better? It was just one of the thousands of words that had fled his vocabulary in the last ten months. But he knew it was a word they needed to hear, and that if they heard it enough times he would be able to leave. He knew where he had to go.

The blackness called him. There was no light left. It wasn't as if there was a struggle left to lose, all life force having deserted him. The last thing he had to do required no energy and no thought. It would be over, and he would never again have to think about it. That was the only strange thing about it, there being no other side to it; no later. Everything else had a later and was laden with the baggage of so many words needed for description and evaluation. Too many words for a man with a fatally wounded vocabulary.

He looked in the mirror and realised that he had not seen the person looking back at him for nearly a year. He didn't feel sorry for this man, instead wondered vaguely whether the emptiness he felt was created by terminally wounded words all over his life, poking out of the ground like lexicographical memorials. The pills they had given him were neatly lined up on the glass shelf above the tap that ran into the basin, steaming already from the hot water swirling around it.

When he cut, he cut lengthways. This was one of the benefits of spending so much empty time in a mental health facility. He had seen the scars of people who knew how to cut, but clearly not how long and deep to make their incisions.

He could not remember any pain but had strong memories of the heat of the water on his wrists and lower forearms. There was also a sense of waiting.

He had not been aware of the blackness, either then or the next time. Pondering now, from what should have been some other side, he wondered if there actually was any blackness, or if there was, in fact, only light which continued in an endless stream.

The psychotherapist who occasionally visited him and sat by his bed seemed fascinated by the blackness and appeared disappointed to hear this theory that it probably did not exist. He had mused over this with a brogue shoe crossed over a corduroyed leg, sucking the arm of his glasses as he distanced himself from this view. It was as if he knew about the blackness and thought you clearly had to experience it more than twice, and for longer than the standard resuscitation period, to really get acquainted with it.

The therapist left, and as the door swung closed after him a nurse entered with his meal tray. It was the same nurse who had tended him during the five days he had spent in hospital since regaining consciousness this time around. He recalled that last time he was here his nurse had been a stark, judgemental woman who seemed to resent reeling him back into a life he had chosen wantonly to abandon.

Each time this latest nurse brought in a meal it was accompanied by fifteen to twenty words of his lost vocabulary. The words stayed in the room with him after she left, a peculiar foreign language he had not used for almost two years. She did not treat him like a ward number or a clip chart entry. Her behaviour made it clear that she had no expectations of him. She even seemed to like him.

As she put the tray down he followed her professional gaze to the dressings on his wrists. Her eyes met his but he saw no pity there. In its place were questions, but also a recognition tantamount to connection. He realised he had seen it before in her, but this time it was accompanied by a mischievousness he could not yet place.

'Do you have me wired up so you can get early warning of me having hurled myself off or at things?' he asked her, borrowing the mischievousness for a sentence. It felt nice there.

'I must be the talk of the Suicide Watch,' he added. 'How do you normally treat the weirdos?'

'Oh, we have a sweepstake,' she said. 'I have Thursday. If you're still alive on Wednesday night I'll leave you a knife on your tray when I go off shift.'

He smiled. He knew that in saying this, joshing with a patient, she had taken a risk, more personal than professional, and was grateful to her on more levels than she would ever understand.

At that moment, in his mind, a rope appeared at the bottom of the well. He placed both of his hands around it. He wondered if it led out of the darkness.

She pottered around him for a while, tapping things, writing stuff down, emptying something, and as they chatted she offered him more of his lost vocabulary.

'It's a terrible thing to lose a child.'

He nodded. She let the words rest there for a while. She seemed to be doing more jobs around the room than usual; as if she was waiting for something. He realised that he had been waiting for something too, and talked to her about some of the pain. A part of him realised it was the first time he had connected with himself or anything he was feeling in the two years since his daughter had died.

The tapping and writing over she stayed to talk with him further. Her eyes never left his face. When she said something it was real. He ran his fingers over the edges of his bandages as he talked. After twenty minutes she told him that she had to go. There were other patients in different rooms on the ward. He thanked her for staying with him. As she left she said she would pop back in and see him after the end of her shift.

That night he talked to her through the numbness. He wondered if it was the drugs, but didn't care. Four hours later she went home. It seemed funny to him that he felt as if he could still see her even when all the lights in the room were off, apart from those bouncing off the bottom rail of his bed from the monitors behind where he lay.

That night he had found out that if he tugged on the rope at the bottom of the well it would still hold firm.

Four years later he could still see her but there was, perhaps, a little too much light behind her.

'We might have to wait a while for this one,' he said, 'the sun is still behind you and is causing a real glare on the lens.'

She adjusted the little girl on her knee a fraction, enough to keep steady as she glanced over her left shoulder.

'We can do it later. Why don't you come and sit down for a couple of minutes.' He looked tired, she thought. It was as if a part of him felt he had to cram all of his life into every moment. Even on this, their first real holiday as a new family, expectation seemed to queue to fill every moment. It was exhausting to watch him. He placed the lens cap back on the camera and stood looking at them thoughtfully for a while. His face was much more full now and had caught the early May sun in pink patches on both cheeks. This first bloom of a tan darkened the blue of his eyes which in turn softened the way he looked at her. His smile stopped suddenly.

'You aren't sitting too far back, are you?'

She suddenly became conscious of the well cover pressing against the back pockets of her jeans.

'They said it is completely safe. The cover is almost brand new so there's nothing that can happen. It must be about three feet thick.'

He gave her that look again. He had given it to her so many times in the past four years that she had begun to feel it was as much a part of her life as his. That was fine, she had known all she needed to know, and they had invested an immense amount of time building compartments for him to keep his memories safe and real. He wandered across to them and sat down right back on the cover. She knew that he was placing himself in a position that would enable him to sacrifice himself and push the two of them to safety if the unimaginable happened. How could she tell him that it wouldn't? It already had, hadn't it?

She looked across the walled garden to the tower. It was a truly magical place. He had promised her a castle for their little princess and this wonderfully extravagant folly delivered. The ground floor was almost entirely windowless, which seemed to exaggerate its strong red bricks raising to an arcaded parapet on the roof itself. The polygonal buttresses punctuated the four corners of the building rising to turrets three floors above. From here she could see the room in which the three of them had spent last night, and could imagine the tiny spiral staircase revolving throughout the building to each of the rooms, one per floor, which were to be their base for this precious week.

The reason he had chosen the folly was because of the well on which they were now perched. She did not entirely understand why, but she had seen his letter asking the Trust to specify its exact dimensions and degree of restoration. She had also seen the replies to him that had reiterated an assurance of total safety.

For him, sitting on top of this well with his family brought him back into the light. He could no longer see the rope that had hauled him here, or feel its coarse fibres against his hands. He didn't need to. The fact of his sitting on the well's vertex meant that he no longer needed it.

But what of the journey? Sitting here with an arm around his wife's shoulders, looking down into the face of his daughter, he recalled a conversation at the end of a cold, leaden winter. It was with a friend he had not seen for four years. The friend had visited him in hospital when he had no time for friendship. But this man would not let go. Christmas cards, the occasional email and text messages had kept fragile lines of communication open. But what had hustled them into their first meeting in all of this time had not been his need to speak to his friend about matters of history, but his friend's need to talk with him about affairs of the present.

Their late lunch had started with a plate of garlic focaccia which they dispensed in accompaniment with the prospects of rain, Champions League results and the shape of the new three series. A side salad they hadn't ordered arrived and was viewed with a suspicion typical of men who had not the slightest intention of doing anything with something as pointless as rocket salad and a chopped onion.

'She left me. It's all gone tits up.'

He looked at his friend. This wasn't a huge surprise. He had not caught up on the relationship in nearly half a decade, but this news was consistent with what he knew of the rhythm of their marriage.

'Have you asked her why she left?' he asked. It was a question that might have seemed reasonable between two other people.

'No.' His mate across the table picked up the beat of the conversation instantly. To him it had been a foolish question in the context of their friendship and he was surprised to hear it. He continued.

'She is too busy making sunshine with Boat-boy. But she says she doesn't want any of the money, and that it is all for the best. Oh, and that I am to move on, you know. Bollocks. She said it was always going to happen. It just happens to be now.'

As he said this his friend wondered what was different about the man in front of him. He supposed that 20 million had to buy you something new, but couldn't quite place exactly what it was. His friend's hair was still a shocking ginger, but less gelled these days; maybe that was it. Or maybe it was something else.

Returning to their conversation, he realised it was true. He had known their marriage would never work. There was something missing. When he had seen them together it was like watching two actors reading for different plays. They said things in turn, but missed the beat of intimacy he had once shared with his first wife. In truth, he had always known his friend's marriage would fail. This had been a conversation in the waiting. He tried another tack.

'Is it a terrible thing?'

'What do you think?'

'I think it may not be a terrible thing.'

'How can you say that? Jeez, man, you sound like my therapist!'

Therapist? *Therapist?* his friend thought. That's a change, maybe that was it. And maybe it explained their meeting here. But it was not the time for that. There was something else.

'I can say it because I know about terrible things.' With anyone else that would have been a trump card he should not have played. With this particular friend it was no such thing; it was just the thing he wanted to say.

'How can her leaving me not be a terrible thing?'

This was the moment, his friend realised. He had not realised it right up until the moment arrived, and suspected that sometimes you never knew about such moments even after they turned up, and perhaps even when they had long passed. Sometimes you probably never knew about them at all. But this was the moment. He had no doubt of it.

'Because we are not designed to know. It's not what happens.' He flattened his hand and pushed it right up against his face, so that the back of his hand would have obscured his friend's view of much of his face. The palm of his hand was pressed up in front of his own eyes.

'You know, when this is the view of your life you cannot see anything else. There is no perspective. You can only see things close up and, as human beings, we make judgements there and then about the horror of what we see and what we don't. Everything is terrible and we think there is no way out of it.

'It is only when you see it all from a distance that you realise different things. One of those things is that you could not possibly have seen them differently before, and you were not supposed to.'

His friend looked at him, aghast. 'So, what, this is God or someone doing this? We put up with all the shit because some omniscient being has some perspective we don't have?'

'What if it is not God? What if it is *we* who are designing it all? And what if we are doing it all from a different perspective with many more dimensions, it's just that when we see it in a single dimension it appears to be shit? *We* are the designers, and we are designing ourselves to learn.'

'Learn what?'

'Patience, relativity… hell, I don't know. What if all we have to learn is that we have to learn?'

'I think the lessons could be a bit more gentle, even more focused,' his friend retorted. 'I mean, Jeez, we need an agenda here!'

'Why?' He was getting excited now. 'Because then all we would learn is that lessons are gentle? This is the real stuff.'

'Shit, man, your kid died. How real do you want to get?'

'But what if that isn't the reality?' He was getting excited now. This was what he had come to feel. 'What if death isn't what we think? Consider what wouldn't have been if that had not happened. Think about my now. What about my *now*?'

Somewhere out in the universe an immense string of light sprayed up from behind a planet, as a star shifted, announcing the end of an eclipse. Where there had previously been blackness, the star having been completely occluded by this planet, there were now streams of luminous intensity creating definition and shadows where there had been no places before.

It had taken its time, but now he was aware this is how it had to happen. The judgement and crying and screaming had been like the hand up against his face.

At that moment their pizzas arrived. The tomato sauce bubbled over crispy chillies and oven scorched pepperoni. They had ordered them with an extra topping of soft egg. They looked good. Right now their pizzas looked good.

Just five hours before these pizzas had arrived with their errant side salad, another man burst out of a door on a tube station twenty miles away. The train had taken an age to stop. Then the hopelessly inept driver took what seemed like an hour to align the inside doors with the sliding glass gates at the edge of the platform.

'Come on, come *on!*' the stricken traveller had mouthed, stabbing a look towards the front of the train where he knew this driver would be sitting balanced over a lever and an early evening paper. Then, through quarter opened doors, he propelled himself off the train and made for the exit.

Gathering speed, he bowled past three people on the platform who had decided to consult each other on something compelling, standing uselessly in exactly the place where he needed to wheel in order to make his way towards ground level and the mainline station. He aimed his bag to push one against another like kissing billiard balls snug together in their triangle; the first tourist break in a new spring frame.

He got to the escalator and allowed himself the luxury of wrenching his sleeve back to reveal the leering face of his watch. *Three minutes until his train left.* Mounting the steps two at a time, the traveller breathlessly calculated the odds: a minute to the barriers, another one up the final stairs and onto the station concourse, and one more to locate the right platform. He could still do it. He had to do it, they had given him no option. This was not just a deadline; it was a non-negotiable, once only, be there, get sharp, take it or leave it, final chance, no excuses, '*Do you want this or not?*', life-changing opportunity.

The conspiracy has started at the tube station when the machine had refused his credit card, leaving him at the mercy of a queue to the ticket office made up entirely of people with old timetables, all the time on earth and no knowledge of how the system worked. To make matters worse, the man in front of him at the ticket machine, a master commuter, had slid his banknote into it and had it instantly welcomed at precisely the time he had most needed this to happen. To the traveller's chagrin, his fellow commuter had then glided up the stairs towards his mainline platform.

As the master commuter reached the top of the stairs he stopped, turned and looked directly at his fellow traveller now stuck in the queue. They did not recognise each other, had never met and never would. The traveller stopped glaring at his watch and looked up, blinded by a moment he wouldn't remember and would never understand even if he had. He saw this master commuter, a man with ginger hair and the look of purpose, shake his head three times and then turn to walk out of his sight and towards the mainline platform overground.

All of this took less than three seconds. Then, for the traveller with a non-negotiable date with destiny, the nightmare continued, in the ticket queue and down on the platform where the monitor remained studiously innocent of destinations or departure times, all this compounded by a passenger emergency on the train in front of his.

Now, just 2½ minutes away from what felt like the end of hope, he bounded up the final six steps of the escalator, virtually leapfrogged a child who had strayed too far from the skirts of her mother, and launched himself at the automatic ticket gates.

He jabbed at the slot twice, three times, four. Each time the machine cried out 'Assistance Required'. He shot a look across at a large ticket officer whose attention had been grabbed by the serial ringing of the barrier alarm.

'Can I help you?' this huge, ponderous uniformed man asked of the manic-looking customer with bloodshot staring eyes that stared wildly at him with plaintiff loathing. 'Sir,' he added.

'Let me through!' the man enjoined. 'Look, I have a perfectly valid ticket.' He thrust the little square rectangle of cardboard too close into the officer's face.

'Let me see, sir.' The ticket officer reached into one of two breast pockets for his reading glasses. They were fairly new, and the habit of wearing them had not yet formed. Not there... he patted on the other one. No shape like reading glasses registered against his hand. He tried the first pocket again.

The man at the barrier made a kind of yelping noise, more than a squeal but not yet a scream. 'Come on, come on!' the yelp tried to say.

Glasses located, the ticket officer looked at this banshee traveller over them. This was new to him. He liked the feeling of wearing glasses. It gave him a sense of, I don't know, authority. He looked into the glowering red eyes of the man at the barrier, pushed away the ticket held to his face and took it.

'This is fine, sir.' He reached into another pocket where he knew, this time, he would certainly find his pass card. He let this maniac through the barrier.

The maniac tore through the ticket hall and up the final steps, arriving panting on the station concourse. He stared wildly up at the departures monitor. He was searching for the 8.12. Nothing. There were three other trains up on the board that had been due to leave ten minutes or more before his. But his wasn't there. He looked for a clock amidst the information being offered there. It was 8.13. He hurtled towards the platform his train would normally leave from. He saw it, doors closed, inching out of the station. He threw himself at it. Electronic door locks! The train moved out. He had missed it by less than three seconds.

He threw his briefcase onto the platform, trembling with rage. He swore loud and long, saw a startled early commuter look at him from under the monitors on the concourse, and swore again.

That was it, then. It was over. His big chance, gone. He could ring them but it was pointless, useless. The timing of the meeting had been non-negotiable.

It was then the artificial conversations started circling in his brain. He could hear his girlfriend saying to him later, 'It's all for the best'… 'There'll be other chances.' There would be worthless talk of other ships on the ocean, pebbles on the beach, olives in the fucking jar.

The manufactured conversations began spiralling towards the blackness in the middle of his mind. He would not be consoled out of this one by the prosaic vacuousness of well-meaning people with positive attitudes, armed with endless stories of new beginnings and happy endings. There was no one sitting on a cloud in the universe looking after his best interests.

They could all just *fuck off*.

He knew better. What was bad, was bad. Silver linings were for clouds carrying aircraft in the London Heathrow holding pattern over Berkshire. This was just bad. It wasn't judgement or perspective; it was sheer bloody *fact*.

Fifty-five minutes later the 8.12 pulled into its destination station dead on time. Forty seconds after it arrived, a workman on the roof of the station slipped on some wet lead flashing and, scrabbling for purchase, jammed his leg through the ceiling. This dislodged a murderously jagged slab of plaster which then fell from the roof onto the concourse below, smashing down onto a place where no one was standing, or walking or rushing for a taxi. Others emerging from the 8.12, who were around and close to the place where the plaster had impacted into the floor, were to tell people in their lives that this had been a very near thing for them. A narrow escape.

At 3.08 that day two other people, a couple, were heading back into London on the M3. He had said that she could drive back. Well, actually there wasn't a great deal of choice involved in either the negotiation or the decision, as he had drunk three glasses of wine over lunch. It was his way of dealing with their visit to what he still endearingly called 'the nut house'.

She hadn't drunk any wine, even though one glass would have enabled her to think less obsessively about the side salad she had ordered but which had failed to arrive. She also badly needed to forget the reason for their trip out of town that day. Her friend had gone for ever, she realised that now. Her husband had told her to say goodbye to her before, but it just wasn't the time. Now it was time.

She had short-circuited the discussions and volunteered to drive before the wine was ordered. She loved driving, but didn't much like driving with him.

There were only two things they argued about: her driving because it was wrong, and his driving because it was right. As they passed the exit to Woking and Camberley she glanced across at him. The wine had hit the spot, he was sleeping and she started to relax into the rhythm of the journey. She needed to forget their visit and focus her attention on the future. She was sure it was what her friend would have wanted for her.

It was like peace entered the vehicle through the air vents. This was an essential part of her progress, to not only find the source of her peace but how to tap into it through conscious effort. She focused on turning some of the obsessive thoughts from the visit into shapes she could squeeze out of her mind.

Her attention on the rear lights of the car in front of them was momentarily distracted by one automatic sweep of the wipers smoothing away April rain droplets from the windscreen. Gathered together, they then ran down the rubber blades spilling onto the waxed bonnet of the car, which they used as a springboard onto the road. The sun was now out and ushered afternoon warmth into the car, the first of the spring.

She had realised that peace was not about geography, but decision. It was not a place you could go to which you recognised because the pieces fit and the shades of colour were just right. It was the last in a series of choices that ultimately defined who you were.

She knew it was what she most wanted, but to want it sent out a message of hankering and need, not peace. It was not about the chronology of change but the consequence of decisions made in real time.

She glanced across at him again. He didn't get it. He said that it was fine to yearn for something greater, but everyone needed 'real objectives'.

Peace, he had sneered, was for old fat people who could afford to sit by pools at the end of their lives being waited upon by others who would never be able to afford it for themselves, assuming they lived long enough.

No. No, *no*, she had thought. You cannot find peace in a brochure and book two weeks there, extending it by paying for a flight upgrade on the journey out. In the same way that you cannot find it in the bottom of a glass, or on the debit side of a bank statement.

It's a place inside which is calling you home.

These were her thoughts as they made their way up the motorway. They were thoughts that belonged to her and to share them was to invite repudiation and other people's traumas. One of these other people lay sleeping in the passenger seat beside her. He stirred as they approached the sign declaring they were two miles from the M25.

'Which way are you going back?' he asked her, more awake than he should have been at this stage in his afternoon soporiferous state. Her hands tightened slightly on the steering wheel. He wouldn't have noticed.

'I think through central London,' she answered, 'I don't want to risk the motorway.'

'Hmm,' he said 'the Hammersmith flyover at half four in the afternoon.' It could have been a question, maybe a statement. More likely an accusation-in-waiting. Peace started floating out of the vehicle through a small hole just under the accelerator pedal.

'We agreed that if I drove you would let me choose the route home,' she said.

'OK, OK, it is your choice. I was just thinking...'

Well, don't,' she snapped 'I'm fine. It's fine. The journey is *fine*.'

'Fine,' he said.

She loved him, of course. He was part of her journey and, she was sure, her destination. He may not share all of her thoughts and she knew that part of his function as a partner, friend, and of course a *man*, was to tug her chain, enabling her to explore her own boundaries and make different decisions in relation to them. She had even shared this with him. This had resulted in times when, at his most exasperating and, as she struggled to be positive, he would look at her.

'Tug, tug,' he would say, grinning. Sometimes she grinned back; at others she plotted his death.

She ploughed on beyond the M25 exit and blessed the clear run past Sunbury Cross at junction one. He seemed to sleep fitfully as they went through Twickenham, bypassed Chiswick and literally flew over Hammersmith Broadway. She felt her tension ease again and, as she always did no matter how often she saw it, strained through the windscreen to see the copy of Victoria's imperial crown on the lantern above the central cupola of the Victoria and Albert Museum as they drove through South Kensington. All of her decisions were flowing in the right direction when he flicked open an eye.

'Which bridge?' he said.

'What?' She had heard him perfectly well. It had previously been a point of some contention between them.

'Which bridge?' he persisted.

'Let me surprise you,' she tried.

'Can I just make a suggestion?'

'No. You can't "just do" anything. You never actually just suggest. You want to control the journey and, hey, look – *I'm* driving.'

He looked at her, seeing a vein on the side of her neck pulsing. 'Tug, tug,' he said.

She wondered briefly about what garrotting would feel like at the hands of the garrotter. A quiet settled between them. It was not particularly comfortable, like an un-negotiated peace. But it enabled her to drive past the magnificent Hyde Park Hotel and head up towards Wellington Arch.

This was too much for him.

'*Which bridge?*' he said, sitting upright in his seat. He tugged boisterously at the lateral and reclining seat controls as he boggled his eyes out of the window, in disbelief at what he clearly thought were foolishly out of place landmarks in the wrong part of London.

She fortified herself, realising that she was now forced to reveal her route.

'I'm not going over a bridge, I've decided to head for the tunnel via the Embankment.'

It was a point of contention between them. He would cross the Thames and then cross back to reach the Limehouse Link Tunnel; she had chosen to get there a different way.

'*What?*' he yelled. 'That's insanity. The Embankment at this time of day. Why? *Why?*' He had lost it, he was screaming at her.

'Look,' she said 'we agreed that I would drive and so I could choose the route through London. So bog off and butt out.'

However, he was neither in the bogging nor butting mood. She felt that she could not reveal her real motivation for the route she had chosen. For her there was something truly uplifting about Parliament Square and the Palace of Westminster. When alone, she would always drive this way through London. The magic of the early evening light being absorbed by a hundred of Sir Charles Barry's mini honeyed Gothic towers, glowing gold in psychedelic detail and reflecting off the Thames, was fuel to her.

It was her favourite building, even worth braving the traffic for. But not for him. As fate conspired to slow their progress alongside the river, he sucked his teeth and kept a running commentary about the stupidity of her decision. She kept her chain just out of reach of his tugging hands, but it was a struggle made worse by the jams around Blackfriars with worse still to come by the time they snailed down Upper Thames Street.

'Fifteen minutes thirty-five seconds,' he said. He had pushed the button on the stopwatch function of his watch at Parliament Square and was determined to give her a minute by minute update of precisely how much of his life she had chosen to waste by making the unforgivable decision to drive home via a pretty route.

The number got greater as they crawled past Tower Bridge, finally hitting The Highway at a time it was least willing to live up to its name.

They joined a queue for the Limehouse Link Tunnel at 'twenty-five minutes fifteen seconds' and waited there. The only sounds in the car were his reading out of numbers and her attempts at breathing control. Her feelings of peace on the M3 were another lifetime ago.

'I think the tunnel is closed,' she finally managed when they had been stuck there for another quarter of an hour. It was a statement of truce, but he was on the winning side and had no intention of letting it go.

'I would have been here forty minutes ago,' he observed. There it was again, another sharp tug on the chain. Tug, bloody tug, she thought.

He tugged. 'You and your positive bloody thinking! Go on, make something good out of this. Seeing the sunset on the river, looking at the lovely buildings on the way; making us late home. It's just sheer bleedin' insanity. Nonsense, it is, all nonsense.'

She contemplated her choices. I can choose peace rather than this, she thought.

She looked out of the window at the rain. The tunnel had been cordoned off and they were painfully edging their way towards a police diversion. A number of officers in reflective yellow jackets were busying themselves with bollards, barking into walkie-talkies as they pointed menacingly at cars who crept out of the patterns the police made on the road.

As they waited an officer came within hailing distance. She let down the driver's window.

'What is the problem, Officer?'

'Accident in the tunnel,' he replied, 'carnage – we have dead 'uns all over.'

She felt a chill. They were so near to the entrance of the tunnel; it felt that death was very close.

'God,' she said, 'how dreadful! When did it happen?'

'Oh, about forty minutes ago – some maniac in a van took out two cars, then hit a wall.'

The sentence and the number hung between husband and wife in the car. They drove the rest of the way in silence and, at last, parked the car in the underground garage. As they walked up the stairs to the lift he took hold of her hand.

'What are you thinking?' he asked her.

'I was wondering what you were thinking,' she replied.

He seemed to give it real thought.

'You know how you say that you are the designer, do you think you designed that?' he jerked his thumb in the general direction of the Limehouse Link.

'What, the accident?' she asked him, genuinely surprised by his question.

'No, the fact that we weren't in it.'

'Have you ever thought that perhaps you designed that part?' she said.

'So what, I can design this stuff by accident?'

'What if the only place that accidents occur is in this tiny little three-dimensional perception of ours? What if we both learn to trust ourselves and what we can achieve a little bit more?'

He took a deep breath. He had never asked her about this stuff before, even though they both knew it was so important to her, redefining her life, even.

'So, you believe that something galactic and intelligent and celestial designed us to be late.' He took a breath. 'Forty minutes late at the tunnel?'

She looked at him. Wasn't it amazing that you can share a bed, a takeaway carton, a toothbrush, even socks with someone, and they still didn't know you...

'No,' she said.

He looked at her as she watched the numbers on the lift panel in front of them descending. Countdown.

'You believe that it wasn't the universe. It was us, wasn't it? Some part of us did it? A part that we can't get to, but which can always get to us?'

'What if there is no separation between us and what we know as the universe? So one thing cannot make a decision for another thing? It's all us.'

'So now we are the universe?' he asked her.

Maybe he knew her after all. The lift was close to them. 'Yes,' she said.

'You're one very weird lady,' he said, 'but I guess that's why I let you love me.'

The lift arrived and he pulled on her hand.

He grinned at her. 'Tug, tug,' he said.

The man, a stranger to himself as well as others around him, shook his head, it didn't help. It hurt. He decided not to do that again, but hoped he would remember not to. He remembered virtually nothing else.

He was outside a shop he didn't know in a street he couldn't place. He was trying to work out where he was and why he might be there. He shook his head. It hurt.

There was the number again, flashing into his brain from periphery to periphery, taunting him with its incompleteness. He just couldn't catch it but felt it might be a clue. He didn't have a phone with him, but thought that the four digits he was getting could be part of a phone number. He had to remember it; maybe he had to ring it. He found an old piece of paper in the pocket of the coat he felt must belong to him. He was wearing it. Another clue. There was nothing else in the pockets, no money, no keys or wallets containing photographs of smiling children.

The four digits flashed through his mind again. He had the real urge to write this number down. He looked at the shop. It might be a newsagent's, he thought. Going in he saw that it was definitely a newsagent's. He wondered what they did for a living and if any part of the memory he had lost contained that level of information, and if it did what he generally did with it.

There was no one around. No one to ask. There was a carton on the counter above the sweets and beside the strange rectangular pieces of paper in clear perspex tubes claiming to be 'scratch cards'. There was one pen left in the carton.

He didn't remember if he was a thief but realised by his reaction as he ran panic-stricken from the shop that if he was he probably wasn't a very good one. He bumped into a man on his way out and pulled his hat further down over his forehead, so even if he had recognised the man, which he felt he should, then he wouldn't be identified.

He tried to pull the cap from the pen but it was stuck. He had to get the cap off because if the number flashed into his brain now he would need to write it down. He tugged and tugged and eventually it released. He sat down on a concrete bollard outside what may have been a hairdresser's and waited for the number to appear in his head.

Down the road he saw that the man he had bumped into had left the newsagent's looking frustrated. He was still too close to the scene of his crime, and moved on so as not to be caught. He followed the shadows on the road because, for some reason he could not place, he felt that this would jog his memory.

He walked quite a way, but didn't know how far as he couldn't remember any measurements of distance or length. He wondered if distances were the same for people who remembered what they were called as to others who didn't have names for them. The number appeared briefly in his head, but he only got four digits down – 1, 1, 2, 0 – before it was replaced by the word 'right'. He wrote that down, too. It might be another clue.

He came across a fork in the road. It was very strange because although he did not remember any of the area he found himself in he was sure it should not be there. It was doubly strange because the road to the left was bathed in sunshine and the one to the right was almost incandescently gloomy; as if it were actually emitting darkness.

This is where he realised it would be an advantage to recall what it would be like to be fearful, or at least reticent. He was quite sure those emotions must have been invented for a reason, but they just did not occupy any space under his hat.

He looked again at the fork in the road. The sunshine was glinting off the windows of the buildings that lined the road to the left, and it seemed as if the road got wider as it poured into the distance. He had forgotten this was a breach of the laws of perspective, so it failed to register with him and he wasn't troubled by it.

The road to the right was much narrower. There appeared to be no separation between light and shade on any part of it. It was utterly uninviting, and it was the road he chose.

He stumbled against its raddled surface, knocking against large metal objects, some sharp and cavernous with contents that smelt like the armpit of the world. He forged on, mobilised by a combination of instinct and will, never persuaded to even look, let alone walk, back. He had now forgotten that he had forgotten the number that had stopped flitting in and out of his memory. Above him, crows circled under gathering clouds to watch the pathetic fallacy of the late afternoon suffocate any remaining light from the scene. One of the murder of crows alighted on the top rung of a rusty fire escape ladder hanging loose against the blackened brickwork of a derelict warehouse, calling for attention. Picking a careful path over crudely laid paving slabs, the man with no memory instinctively looked up to return the death-black stare of the crow. As he did it was joined by another, and a third, calling in a chorus as he lurched on, falling on the uneven surface of the path he followed. In doing so he fell against a sharp nail sticking out of a piece of wood that pointed back in the direction he had come. The rusty end of the nail tore his jacket as he pulled away from it, ripping open one of the pockets. The piece of paper that had been in there fell out and floated to the ground, where it joined the detritus lying strewn in piles, waiting to be blown into the already overstocked gutters, to rot with the surrounding putrefaction.

Unwittingly, he moved on, quickening his pace, walking further along the dark road which turned into an alley and threatened to become a corridor. A distance behind him a freak gust of wind threw two of the large metal objects against each other and into the road, completely blocking his path back. They landed with a deafening crash, resonating around the closing walls of the buildings that witnessed it. He would have looked back but did not see any point in doing so; it was not where he was going.

He was now squeezing between oily tanks and wooden cartons on both sides of the alley, and banged his head against the remains of another ladder, barren with crows, suspended about twelve inches above him, and hanging away from the wall. Disorientated, he slumped against the surface of a moist green barrel that smelled of fish and held his head. It hurt.

When the pain cleared a little he looked up at his chosen route and saw ahead of him an area where the alley opened up slightly. He headed for it with more enthusiasm than he would have mustered in a place and time where he had memories.

As he reached this open area he saw, under some mud, what appeared to be a blue light shining from the ground. The light seemed to be twinkling and winking at him, even though there was no source to cause it to do so.

He knelt down and examined it. Upon closer examination he could see that the light was actually a brooch. It was an amazing colour, ice blue, shining in this wilderness of dark.

He picked it up and his finger dug into the pin on the back of the brooch, which then sunk into his skin. He pulled his finger away, dropping the brooch back into the mud, and, looking down, he saw that it had drawn blood from a small puncture wound in the centre of his fingertip. He sucked the finger but the blood refused to stop its flow. After a couple of minutes he bent down again and more carefully picked up the brooch. He manoeuvred his grip away from the pin and in doing so the tip of his bloodied finger made contact with the blue stone adorning the brooch.

As soon as contact was made he was transported back.

In the same instant he found himself sitting on a metal seat in a silo sheathed in a material which he surprised himself by thinking had not yet been invented. He looked up towards what may have been an exit. He saw a figure standing a short distance from him. It seemed to be a man. If it was a man, he appeared to be wearing some kind of silver one-piece suit covered in minute scales.

'Welcome home,' the silver man said.

He looked around him. 'This is home?'

The silver man peered into what may have been a gauge. 200,000 generations of genetic engineering made old habits hard to break; he tapped the gauge.

'How is your head?'

'It hurts.' It was also hatless. It must have fallen off somewhere on the journey.

'Hmm. The drug you took to forget the past should be wearing off soon.'

'What past?'

'Well, technically it is this, the present; or to be more exact, it is the future for where you were.'

His head hurt a little more.

'Were you successful?' the silver man asked.

'At what?'

'Did you manage to get hold of the pen before him?'

The man with the bad head realised that attempts at language were not having that much success at the moment and decided on a blank look instead. It had been around so much longer than language and had a better success rate.

The silver man took his cue. 'You sent yourself back in time to stop someone buying a pen in a newsagent's, do you remember? Otherwise he would have bought it, found the cap hard to release, tugged it off with his teeth, swallowed it accidentally and choked to death.'

The blurring was clearing a little but not because of this explanation. The blank look he gave the silver man now was not out of choice, but habit. He managed a question.

'I thought time travel wasn't possible.'

'Try to focus here,' said the silver man, entering the outskirts of exasperation, 'you just stepped out of a time machine. It wasn't possible, but it is now. It couldn't be done in the present, so the future made it possible.'

'But can't it be abused to change the fabric of time, and all that?'

'Well, that's kind of the point. Remember the man's life you saved?'

Again a blank.

'The man in the newsagent's. The one who would have bought the pen.'

'Oh, him. You mentioned him before. Who is he?'

'He will have a daughter whose son's daughter will work with you to programme the machine you are stepping out of only to be used for the purpose you intended when you invented it. It had to work; without your intervention this could all have gone badly wrong.'

The hatless, once forgetful man looked around him. Some parts of this were now coming back to him. The room he was in was suspended inside another much larger one, which appeared to be suspended in four or five more transparently walled rooms extending into what could have been infinity. Something here rang true. There was part of him that knew what this was. But what had the silver man said? That wasn't it.

'You are saying that I made all of those choices in the past in order to make the present work out?'

'All of them.'

'So what, I had no freedom of choice back there; it was all predestined?'

'Oh no, that's not it at all. The choices made for you were made by you, for you. That's ultimate free choice. There is no separation between you and any part of the intelligent universe. You were making the choices. You just learnt to trust yourself, or more probably you unlearnt how not to trust yourself. You remembered who you truly are.'

He knew now. He just had to make sure. 'The road I took, the dark one? The one that appeared to be a bad choice?'

'It was all right, every bit of it. It's just that then you could not see it and now you can. Then you would have been clogged with judgement and other people's choices. You were sending yourself messages that you learnt to trust.'

'The messages came from me in a different time, yes?'

'Yes.'

'And there is no separation between me and the intelligent universe?'

'That's right.' The silver man looked at him, and knew.

'There is no time machine, is there?' He was hatless, but not stupid. A growing part of him knew it was time.

'What do you mean?' The silver man knew exactly what he meant. He also knew it was time.

As the man with no hat started to speak, the outer transparent rooms began to expand upon themselves and merge into those beyond them. See-through walls that had appeared to separate them enlarged and then collapsed, each one revealing the infinity they had masked.

'None of that was real, was it? There is no time machine because there is no need for one. If there is no separation between me and the intelligent universe there is no need to invent something to travel through time. I just sent myself this to learn something.'

The silver man looked at him with eyes that did not belong to any man. There was no longer any need for him to feed the hatless man the conversation.

'And I have learnt. So what is this?'

'This?' said the silver man. 'What do you think this is?'

The hatless man waited. He knew the answer was coming.

The silver man, who was no longer silver or a man, told him. 'This is the place the clues have brought you back to. The end of the learning. When you tell the story of it others will understand their own clues.'

He remembered other things now. 'And the people at the well, the man at the station, the couple at the tunnel? Were they real, or simply part of me sending myself clues to put all this together?'

'Ah, them... No, they're as real as you are. But yes, they are connected to you, sending and receiving clues in the same way as you. They will return as you did, when it is time.'

'And the brooch that brought me back?'

'Another clue for those who receive it. It has been returned. The woman who needs it back will be taking it out of an unmarked envelope about now.'

The hatless man who hurt his head would have shaken it had it still existed. 'None of them will understand this,' he said.

But that was not true. All of them would understand at the perfect time.

The Boundary

She arrived exhausted at the boundary. Although she felt more physically drained than she could ever remember, she was also completely alert. In front of the wall on which she sat, there was a path leading to a broadening expanse of green. She could not see the verdant place where the path opened up, but she knew it to be there. It had always been there, albeit completely uncharted. Despite never having been to this place on the boundary and never heard it spoken of, its existence and its magical attraction was the most certain thing she had ever felt.

Behind her was a cityscape that she recognised only too well. Within it there was exhilaration, desperation and many addresses in between. The person she was at this place on the boundary had been defined by her journey along the myriad roads she knew lay behind the concrete wall punctuating the outskirts of the city.

Some graffiti screamed along a wall only ten metres or so from where she sat, catching her breath, waiting for her next move. 'Goodbye,' it said, underlined by a huge purple zigzag that culminated in the postscript, 'it's been nice.'

Nice, she thought. It had been many things, often all at once, but 'nice'? Her life had been jam-packed with choices, most of which for most of the time she felt had belonged to other people. Reactions, rules, blame, rejection. Everything had needed dealing with, justifying to herself and to those who made it their business. But now the peace she felt at the boundary made her suddenly aware of the chatter of thoughts in her head.

The chatter became lyrical with so many songs that had entered and left her life, written about the frame of mind she indulged in as she sat on the wall. It seemed daft, but words tumbled around her head as if the score of this moment had been prewritten by romantic hacks who had never known her.

'You're at the gateway (babe),' she heard, 'walk away, it's your time, don't look back (babe), it's time to leave, you only have to believe, baby, baby, baby...'

Jeez, she thought, get to the chorus, two more babies and she'd have a crèche!

But right then another line from another song broke in. 'Shoo-wah, shoo-wah, you're more than you could ever know, do, do, do' (something).

But this was just white noise to her. She had a notion there should be something definitive she should be thinking and feeling. Words that could fill this moment, compartmentalise the past, enable her to touch the brim of her cap, look back one more time, turn and just walk away.

She was sure so many movies and books and commercials had busied themselves preparing her for this moment, pretending to tell and sell her things while covertly implanting their wisdom in her head. But as she sat on the wall with the place before her and her life behind, she found she didn't care.

Of course she cared about some of the people in the city settling for the evening into their boxes, or sitting in other boxes (small or long, on their own or with others) travelling to yet more boxes which, after having been there a while, they would leave and travel away from again.

Some of the boxes, black and square atop with one orange eye that solicitously winked at passers-by, carried digital readouts, liquid crystal displaying to passengers in the back of them the amount of money spent on the journey and capturing the exact moment at which it was being spent. Sometimes, as if offering a clue, the two digital readouts said exactly the same – 11:20. Even given this hint, it rarely, if ever, crossed the minds of those who sat in the back of the boxes, dancing all their lives to these digital tunes, that money and time were not projections of truth, but fabricated realities created by a species who instantaneously forgot they had invented them. Instead, they dedicated their very existence to the choreography.

Looking back at the city, it dawned on her that it wasn't that she didn't care, but that she wasn't feeling anything. Well, actually, that wasn't true. She was feeling something huge but had absolutely no idea what to call it. It didn't fit into any of the categories she had prepared and pre-labelled, waiting like empty mental catacombs to receive such feelings.

After a very short while she realised the chatter in her head had stopped. The inner silence this produced was not eerie, it was just new. Whereas previously her thoughts would have been occupied wondering if she was wearing the right shoes for this and what other people were thinking of her, instead there was... this feeling.

She was utterly by herself in a very different way to simply being alone. It wasn't just that there was no one around. There was simply no one. She looked again at the path leading to the green and suddenly, from nowhere, a figure was beside her. The strangest thing was the figure seemed to have no actual presence and no apparent gender; it simply was. Whereas before it just hadn't been at all.

When she glanced away from the figure to the place from which it may have come she found herself looking towards the city. At this moment, through her peripheral vision, the figure became a man. When she looked back to confirm this it was a genderless figure once again.

'Odd, isn't it?' the figure said. She found herself searching for the social rule covering this situation. The chatter returned to her head, looking for words to make sense of this. She found herself wanting to use the word 'benign' to describe the figure, but realised it would be like using the word 'hole' to describe a bagel.

'I know,' the figure sympathised, 'it is difficult.'

She started. Could this weird figure read her thoughts?

There was no response to the question she posed in her head. Instead, it just stood beside her smiling... what would that be, the chatter wondered: 'wistfully', 'encouragingly'?

'I was going more for engagingly,' it said, 'but I find myself at odds with adverbs. Please feel free to choose.'

Without any warning the chatter quietened again. It disconcerted her.

'Sorry,' she said, 'I have absolutely no idea what to say now.'

'You're probably waiting for me to say, "I am the Gatekeeper," or, "Let me introduce myself, I'm a Journeyman, I have come for you,"' the figure said.

She turned back towards the city, as if for inspiration. In her peripheral vision she saw the man sit beside her on the wall and look with her, concentrating hard on whatever it was they were both looking at. Finally she turned her gaze away from the city and looked at it.

'Where do you come from?'

'Here,' the figure said.

She became aware of sifting through her thoughts for the next thing to say.

'You thought I might say, "From where you are going," didn't you?'

But she hadn't thought that. Maybe the figure couldn't read her thoughts after all.

'No, I can,' it said (engagingly), 'I was just kidding.'

She looked back towards the path.

'To go down there…'

'*Why am I here?*' they said almost simultaneously.

'Oh, sorry,' the figure said, 'slightly out of sync there. We need to practise. Try again.'

'To go down *there*?' she asked.

'Oh, OK,' the figure said, 'we're back. Well, would you rather return there?' It pointed at the city.

They both looked back there. She shuddered and the man shuddered with her.

'You know I can never go back.'

'I know,' he said.

And there it was, the truth. She could never go back to the city. With its streets of lights, labyrinth of roads; its sirens, cries, crashes, calls, squeaks and endless streams of people bustling, darting, forging, jostling, dashing. All the verbs careering around her head sketched the city as a place where people rushed to one place in order to spend time calculating when to rush back to, or on to, another. Relentless journeys, deadlines, smart objectives, timetables, forecasts, meetings to set up projects and conference calls to cancel them.

No wonder part of her was screaming.

Here at the boundary she could see it all as if viewing from a platform high above the city. This was a place of contemplation, a place of choice. From her vantage point she could see it all more clearly than she had ever seen anything before, and as she did she almost imperceptibly shifted her thinking as it revolved around an adjusting centre of reality. In doing so she received an image of a man sitting in a hut whose walls burst with hardy and determined buddleia. He too was looking down on the city, writing down words on a piece of paper; words she could read, as if they were part of her thinking. 'I don't know why I am writing still,' the words said, 'but if you ever read them, and I know you will, it is your time. Never doubt, it is your time.'

Were these the words of the figure sitting beside her on the wall? Why would he show her them, rather than just say the words to her? What was the connection here?

She turned her gaze back towards the path. By her side the figure did the same. Why didn't she just get up and walk down the path? she wondered. She now knew that she couldn't go back to the city and she couldn't just sit on this wall.

'You can only go down the path when it is your time to do so,' the figure said.

OK, she thought, helpful.

But she wanted to go, she really, really did. Wasn't wanting it enough?

'Wanting suggests limitation,' the figure said. 'When you think you want a thing, a feeling, a state of mind, you automatically search for something outside yourself you believe is necessary to satisfy that want.' He looked across at the city, then back at her.

'When you want something, it is the *want* that grows,' he went on.

What followed was a time for thought; hers, she realised, not his. At last he continued. 'That is who you are when you are in the city – a person who is always seeking something beyond what and who you believe you are. There is always a need, and when you look beyond yourself to satisfy it, you underscore the belief in your personal limitation.

'But here everything is different. Here there is no need to want anything. The want is pointless.'

'So I have to learn a whole new language to go there?' She nodded her head towards the path.

'No. You have to remember a whole new you. While you are wanting and hoping and wishing, you are someone else. That person is perfect for over there –' it nodded its head towards the city – 'but that person cannot walk down the path.' He sat looking now at the graffiti-embossed concrete wall.

OK, she thought, more helpful. But now she thought her head was going to explode. Although the volume on the internal chatter had reduced there were still voices of concern, circling like vultures. Some of them couldn't believe what they were hearing, others didn't understand it.

If she couldn't *want*, what would she replace it with? She couldn't begin to count the number of things she had wanted in her life so far. She had even wanted to want things sometimes because someone had once said that this gave her something to aim for. To hear that all of this wanting was the barrier to have what she wanted was... what was the word she wanted?

She tore herself away from looking at and thinking about the city. She knew she had to focus. She knew that if she focused she could create the thing she focused upon. How did she know this? She just did. She focused for a while on the expanse beyond the path and visualised how it would feel when she was there.

It felt unbelievably real. She was surrounded by colour, sound, smells, softness, excitement... and what was that? Unity? Togetherness? No, it was *connection*. She was surrounded by connection. Connection with what? Thinking about what it was made the feeling fade. Pushing the words out of her head and focusing upon the feeling surrounding her intensified it.

Time disappeared on the wall as they sat together. It ceased to exist. It wasn't anywhere, because there was nowhere for it to be.

'You're getting better at this,' the figure said to her.

'Maybe,' she said, 'but I'm having problems with my brain.'

'Your brain?'

It seemed to her that, having mentioned her brain, she was bringing up something of inconsequence, like talking about the plate of biscuits on the table at the beginning of the Kyoto Summit.

'Can I help you with your brain?' the figure said, 'you know, offer some information?'

The feeling she had now was as if watching an antiques show on television where the presenter was patiently explaining how the Stuarts used parchment before email was invented. It was an image that flashed through her mind; she just wasn't convinced that she had put it there herself.

'The brain of every human being in the city is a perfect machine. It is ultimately programmable and will do exactly as it is told. If you ask it why you are so bad at something, why you are always late, why your life is so miserable, it will busy itself, using all of its immense power, in the answering of the question. It will set up a list, find reasons to substantiate every item on it, and even attach creativity and full justification as to why the question, with its new-found answer, is the truth.

'Equally, if you ask it about the potential for success in an apparently desperate situation, what you can do about finding a solution, how you can be the greatest version of yourself, it will work on this, finding points of action, grounds for change and the energy required to achieve it. It is possibility thinking.

'Underestimation of the internal language which fuels the brain is the greatest error of judgement human beings never know they make.'

'Is that what I am doing here?' she asked, 'making that mistake?'

The figure regarded her. She had the funniest feeling it was looking through her and that the next thing to be said was the most important so far.

'You are no longer of the city.'

It was not the answer she expected, but it was one she knew he would give the moment before he said it. So where was she? Was she of this wall? Of this place before the path? And if there was no time there was no next, so what had to happen – or had already happened? – for her to be of somewhere else? The figure had said to her that she would go down the path when it was her time to go. With no time, when would that be?

Before she turned around she knew the figure was regarding her again.

'Can I tell you a story?' it said companionably. She nodded.

'This is a story about that house over there.' It pointed to a small building about fifty metres to the right of where they were sitting. She was absolutely sure it had not been there before. She had surveyed the entire area around the path after sitting on the wall, wondering about her options. Yet there it was now, a house on the edge of the boundary in an elevated position, with two large picture windows staring out over the concrete wall and beyond to the city.

'The owner and tenant of that house was also its architect and builder,' the figure went on. 'He designed it to take full advantage of the view of the city. Even though it backs on to the place where the path leads, and there is a large garden at the back of the house that blends seamlessly into the area beyond, there are no windows or doors looking out on or leading to that place.

'He never goes into the area and doesn't even realise that the path leading to it is just over there.' He pointed to the path leading, she knew, to the broadening expanse of green.

'He spends half of his time peering out over the city and the other half reading hundreds of books he has collected about other men's excursions into the uncharted territory reached by the path. He reads them avidly, devouring any and every experience he can get hold of about this place of wonder. A place he hankers after, *wants*, more than anything else.'

She was waiting for the story to continue, at the same time realising it was over. She sat on her own on the wall and watched the house with large windows, wondering if the man inside was staring out over the city or reading his books about the place behind him. Her thoughts were interrupted by a voice.

'Would you like to buy a map?' There was now a man in a uniform standing beside her, his hat pulled down hard over his eyes, as if to protect him from the glare of the sun. He was holding out a small rectangle of folded paper.

'It's OK,' he continued spotting her questioning look, 'it is official. I am from the government – in charge of maps, actually – and I can assure you this is the definitive and authorised map of the region.' He moved his arm stiffly over the area in the general vicinity of the path and beyond, as if mimicking a gesture learnt in a government training session. 'It's very detailed,' he added.

She looked at the map being offered to her and up at the government official.

'I thought the area beyond this boundary was totally uncharted,' she said.

'Oh, it is,' he replied, 'absolutely.'

'So how can there be a detailed map of it? Has anyone actually been there?'

The uniformed man sighed. This was typical of the asinine thinking of the proletariat. They were always questioning the rules, asking for explanations they were not entitled to. In his previous department he had been responsible for sophistry at the highest level. It was there he had learnt how to deal with awkward questions.

'The map comes with the rules,' he explained, 'you don't have to buy the map, but you must take the rules if you are going there.'

'The rules?' she couldn't believe she was hearing this. He sucked his teeth and pulled again at the front of his hat, a nearly unconscious act of pointing out the official braiding around its brim. He increased his uniformed height.

'Well, you could view them more as detailed instructions on how to behave.'

Thoughts entered her head, rampaged across the front of it for a while and then fled. She found herself selecting among them and discovered one she could use as a question.

'What exactly do I need detailed instructions for?'

'Madam,' the uniform was at full height and he was working hard on its breadth, 'two committees sat independently to draft out, debate and consider in full a series of very reasonable directives necessary when travelling to an area such as this, and to this one in particular.'

'But have they even been there?'

'No one has ever been there, madam, but these highly experienced people are members of the government. They know precisely what they are doing and people should listen when they do it.'

Redundant questions lined up to be shot down. She tried one.

'If there were two independent committees drafting these directives, which one eventually wrote the final version?'

You see, he thought, this is why he was qualified to wear a

uniform. There was a government axiom: if you waited long enough you always made your point.

'Both versions appear with the map, madam. They often conflict but are of equal value.' He proffered the map again. She knew that she would find the exact amount of money required to buy it in her pocket. She did, and paid for it. She was looking at it in all of its remarkable detail when she became aware of the return of the figure on the wall beside her.

'Was that all part of your story?' she asked.

The figure looked away from her, but she knew it was smiling. She wondered if it was almost time for her to go down the path.

'All that is left is for you to use the key,' said the figure.

The key, the key, what was the key? She knew she had to focus upon what it was like to already have the key and, indeed, to have already used it. She searched what she already knew for the answer.

Her search took her back to the city. That was where her most recent experience was. Amidst the noise and chaos she dragged the dark pool of her mind for the clue she knew was there. As she sat on the wall she soared above the orange glow of the evening streets, seeing pinpricks of dazzling colour in the form of neons and sports stadia, streams of winking red lights counter-flowing streams of winking white lights as each doggedly made their way in opposite directions, ignoring the fact that the places they simply had to get to were the places their counterparts simply had to get away from.

People merging with the shadows in dark corners, making friends, making music, making life happen for them, determined to ignore the doubts and fear that plagued everything they did. The fear of failure, fear of being alone, the fear of not doing what everybody else was doing in order to make sense of a life everyone else was leading. The doubts that they were living up to expectations, of their family, their society, their own, and the overwhelming doubt that this was not at all what they should be doing with any part of their lives; that, if there ever was a judgement (and this was where the fears and doubts all coalesced), none of this was what they had been designed to do.

And as she searched the streets she discovered images of herself in rooms and buildings all over the city, forging a life, cowering against its stresses, joining the throng and hiding from it in safe places. She saw herself wondering if she was doing the right thing, doubting if she was good enough to do the things she was doing or attempt the things she wanted to do. She saw her fear – fear of being the same as everyone else and the concomitant fear of being different and alone.

Then she saw a woman she barely recognised as her, in a bed in a small room within an imposing old building coated with dirty grey stucco and crumbling cornicing over large dark windows that stared out on to a car park studded with shivering cars sitting in puddles. There was a clock on the front of the building above the main staircase leading to a front door that had been replaced and updated to shout an incongruous message to the world around it. 'This is a cheerful place,' the modern red door cried. 'There is nothing to be afraid of behind me.' The clock above it that remembered doors of old had been stuck for ten years or more with its dial reading 11.20. It surrounded itself with three plaster angels who were still not used to playing their celestial trumpets to an audience sitting damply in a car park.

People stood around the bed of the woman, who may have been her. They seemed concerned. She tried to look into the woman's eyes, but there was nothing to see there. She searched into the mind of the woman, but all she could hear were distant echoes of doubt and fear.

And then she heard the words again, '…it is your time. Never doubt, it is your time.' The words of a poet.

And that was it. That was her clue. She was back on the wall and the figure was looking at her.

'All the doubt and fear,' she said.

'Yes,' it said.

'It is all so sad, so useless.' She paused, realising, and added, 'So unnecessary.'

'Yes,' it said.

'It is what is keeping me, and everybody else, in the city.'

She looked at the path leading, she knew, to a broadening expanse of green. I choose to replace it, she thought and focused her attention entirely on the thought. She chose to replace it with trust. Trust of who she truly was. Against the trust, the doubt and fear instantly receded and she was on the path.

The figure was no longer beside her, it had become part of her as she walked.

Two people trudged up the stairs of an imposing old building. They knew exactly how many steps there were, having climbed them a number of times before. In her mind the woman of the pair counted them as she ascended, jumping the last one before the top to confuse the total. It was raining and her husband had forgotten to bring the umbrella they kept in the boot of the car, which sat miserably in a small pool of oily water on the left-hand side of the car park.

Despite the rain and the chill of the spring day the red door stood open, as if to defy the concerns anybody may have about security. As they walked up the stairs the man checked his watch. He always did, as he climbed the steps, but had long forgotten the origin of this habit.

They entered the lobby, seeing the grand staircase curl upwards on each side of a large reception desk towards a mezzanine landing. The lights were far too bright, frisking every corner of the enormous hallway and chasing away any lingering impressions of darkness. He saw it, as he always did, the netting that hung taught above the desk and below the balustrade that led east and west along the first floor of the building, down through long white corridors.

They signed in and waited for the doctor.

'She won't know you're here today,' he said when he arrived.

The woman nodded and looked down at the rubber weals on the linoleum flooring as they made their way down the corridor. It was probably true, but there was always a reason to come. The worse it got the more she wanted to visit this place, as if to be here and to leave was to fashion an escape for everyone who never drove out through the gates and back to the city.

Most of the doors along the corridor were closed. She strained to hear sounds behind them as she fought her attempts to do so, knowing that to hear what she imagined was going on behind the doors would be another reason not to return.

They passed two nurses squeaking past in rubber-soled shoes seemingly oblivious of the place they worked. Down this corridor only two rooms had their doors open; one of them was disturbingly empty, with bedsheets spread flat over the mattress like soft white tethers. The other was disturbingly occupied by a person wearing what appeared to be bandages around his wrists, staring at a space beside the window at which the curtains were fully drawn back.

They arrived outside the door two along from the end of the corridor, as it disappeared behind floppy plastic doors into an area marked 'Private'.

'She hasn't responded to any form of stimulus,' the doctor said, checking the chart he was carrying.

'Were we expecting her to?' the husband asked.

The doctor looked at him over small rimless glasses. He decided not to answer.

'She has not been distressed for some time,' the doctor said, choosing among his thoughts. 'This is a good sign, it means we have got the medication levels right.'

The door opposite the one in front of which they were standing opened and a nurse emerged carrying a tray. The wife of the couple peered past the nurse to look inside that room. The bed in the room had been made and was standing empty. In the corner beside the bed sat a woman on a chair much too large for her frame. The woman's face had been ravaged by time and life; it was hanging in folds over a skeleton that couldn't wait for death. She was wearing a dressing gown hopelessly too big for her, and staring bleakly out of the room with piercing bright blue eyes that had seen sunshine and hope before this place. She settled her stare on the female of the trio outside her door.

The woman in the corridor let out a shiver as she stood transfixed by the gaze of this patient. She had the sudden conviction she was seeing herself in fifty years. Her life gathered up and accelerated towards this room. All the hopes that she had now, gone; the dreams and fantasies becoming only distant memories in one heartbeat of time. Through the old woman's eyes she saw her future and knew that it had to be different. There was someone she needed to look back upon and know she had been.

It hadn't yet happened for her; there was everything to do and to be. She was rooted to the spot as her husband gently touched her arm to bring her back to them.

'Tug, tug,' he said softly, only to her, knowing how hard it was for his wife to be there.

The doctor led them into the room of her friend. They all stood at the bottom of what appeared to be an oversized bed containing a small inert figure. The woman of the couple experienced the second strange feeling of her day. It was as if they were looking at a body, as if identifying it. Her husband watched his wife, wondering what she was feeling. He knew it was hard for her. He just didn't know how hard.

'Where is she?' his wife asked in a voice so tiny she wasn't sure if the question hadn't stayed inside her head.

The doctor turned his professional gaze on her. Her husband switched his attention to the view from the window which revealed the driveway twisting out of sight, as if the answer could, in some way, be found out there.

'This isn't her, there is nothing of her in here,' she continued.

'She is still showing signs of cognisance. She responds to light and some sounds. She has retained her swallow reflex and there is every chance that, at some level, she is even aware of our presence.'

The doctor was ticking these points off on slim fingers that had never lightly touched the arm of his patient, leaning across to her as they laughed together during a conversation. The fingers had never intertwined with hers on a sandy path in front of fir trees that led to their secret place on the beach. The fingers had never brushed away the crumb of a croissant from her cheek as she animatedly described a conquest at work over breakfast.

Instead the fingers curled around a pen that wrote prescriptions for L-tryptophan and meperidine, drugs that sent her further away from them, while imprisoning her in this bed.

'You make her sound like a motion-operated waste disposal. But she's not, *she's* not. She is a person, a living being, a soul drowning in drugs…'

As the doctor turned away from this patient to regard somebody he clearly thought could well be his next, the eyes of the woman in the bed opened and looked out into the room. This was the first time she had done this for more than six months.

Her friend stared past the doctor and saw this happening. For her this was the final sign, a clue to everything that was taking place in this huge old monolith of a building. She knew that this was not the woman she had known for more than thirty years. These were not her eyes; they were pale, lifeless replicas.

'She is not here,' she said as her friend's eyes closed again. Neither of the men had seen this happening. It hadn't been for them, it had been for her. It was time to go.

She left the room and walked back up the corridor. Her husband joined her after a few seconds; the doctor didn't follow.

They walked together back out through the red door and across the puddle-strewn car park to where they had left their car. They would have lunch first, and then back to London. She drove them slowly down the drive for the last time. She noticed that some of the grounds were really beautiful. The first tight buds of spring were clinging to the end of branches that appeared to welcome this new life with a deferential bow.

On the last corner before the gates she pulled in beside a concrete wall to allow more room for an oncoming car and they waited momentarily while it passed. She looked out of her window and saw a path which led to a broadening expanse of green.

She pulled out again and drove them back to the city.

The Return

It was a situation he recognised but could not quite place. He knew he had made a choice, but now could not recall the other options. In the place where he knew this a part of him recalled it was normal not to remember.

He was trying to think back to what it was like to be human. As he did a voice was with him.

'It will feel like home.' The voice came from within him, but was already starting to separate, to move away.

'Remind me, what are humans like?'

'Well, you co-designed them,' the voice said. It was now beside him. 'What do you think?'

'Co-designed them?' The feeling of struggling to place facts was unusual. 'Did I?'

'How could you not?'

'I suppose so.' The blocks, like Tetris shapes, were descending into slots in his memory. Part of him didn't want to leave; he wanted to stay. It had been, he wasn't sure how to measure it, having no concept of time, a 'long time' since he had felt anything like this. What would that be called? A month, two years? A lifetime? More?

'It will be over in a... click of the fingers.' They both moved their attention to where fingers could be. There were none there, of course; what possible use would they be? He thought it would seem odd having them again. He'd had them before. He found himself speculating that he was about to spend the next few months just looking at and playing with them, making shadows with them and wondering what they were. There was something magical about this level of simplicity.

'Click of the fingers, eh?'

Of course, it could never actually be 'over', in the same way it would never properly 'begin'. Going from being where there was no meaning to time, to a place where it appeared to everyone that time was an inbuilt non-negotiable weave of the fabric, was part of the strangeness.

He knew he had chosen to go; that was why he was here, preparing to leave. Already his thoughts were separating from the others, and it appeared they had started to work in tenses and verbs.

'They're not, you know,' the voice again.

'What?' he asked.

'Separate from us, your thoughts. They cannot and never will be separate. How could they be?'

'You're starting to communicate in tenses, too.'

'No, it is just you starting to receive your thoughts in them. You are thinking in terms of time.

'Your choice to go there is and was perfect. Humans are perfect, despite the fingers.' Levity; the perfection of levity.

The voice continued, 'So, you have allowed yourself some clues on this journey. What have you chosen?'

It had been like this before. As he got closer to leaving he knew the design was gently inserting more blocks into the universal knowing. It had to be this way, and he knew the odd feeling he was experiencing was a symptom of this. He also realised the moment of departure was drawing nearer, as 'odd' and 'strange' were not things we can feel. Or was that, 'we *could* feel'? The tenses again.

Ultimately it was the experience of this, and so many other things, that was the reason for going, and he knew he would stop knowing this soon. Right now, though, he remembered other clues on other journeys appearing like flashes on the periphery of his consciousness, momentarily hinting at another reality.

Moments (what were they? Nano-somethings – seconds, flashes, whispers?) passed where the vivid picture frames of life dissembled, revealing the truth, and suddenly the life he was leading seemed unreal. Or was it that something else seemed more real? It was as if that moment in time was sliced in two and he could see through it, around the edge, into somewhere else. In the next instant, it reassembled, and the being he was in the life he was leading explained away the moment on a dizzy spell, drinking at lunchtime, a bad prawn… and the solid reality of living on a three-dimensional planet would continue.

Now, as a traveller preparing to leave again, he recalled another journey and another hint. It was as if he was standing and staring at a solid wall that reflected his existence back to him. Suddenly, in the breath of a second, he slipped sideways, as if surfing the crest of a moment, catching a glimpse of the trillions of individual slats which, when viewed from a front-on perspective, made up the impenetrable aggregate of life.

Through the slats was pouring light, music, colours, truth. He saw it all in the moment until he shifted back into position and the hallucination of the slats once again fell into place. The solid reality of life returned.

These clues were scattered, like diamonds awaiting a reflecting light, around the universe. Some were brighter, daring the observer not to see them, others nestled in the dark folds of dimensions.

He recalled, on another journey, a time when he was walking on a beautiful day with the sun behind him. Suddenly in front of him were two shadows, stretching away from his feet. Taken aback, he looked about at the shadows defining the other shapes around him. Each shape spawned only one shadow lazily emanating from its source, while discreetly keeping its distance.

But he had two. He checked behind him for the angled reflection of sunlight from an open window, throwing a roving ray at him as he walked. But there were no buildings with reflecting surfaces, no mirrors on poles, no structures and no earthly reason for the two ethereal hims reaching out, regarding him from the pavement.

He remembered walking quickly away from others in the area, embarrassed they would spot this phenomenon that signposted him as different to them. The shadows hurried with him and then, as he watched, they gingerly merged into one and slowed as he did, before disappearing altogether into a cloud.

All were clues that signalled his connection, reminders of who he truly was; clues missed by him and the billions around him as they replaced the most perfectly simple for the complexity of what they all ironically called 'life'.

Back now in a time that was beginning to exist. 'What?' he said, forcibly re-engaging himself. The forgetting was accelerating. They were now down to about 300 primary colours, flattening and reducing before them.

'The clues? What have you chosen for this journey?'

He was to send himself a message that could, if it was received, enhance the level and type of experiences he would have on the journey. Being who he was, and still having fading memories of previous experiences, he knew he would forget he was the designer and think himself merely part of the design or, more probably, a complex but genetically induced accident. The clues had to be simple. He wanted them to enhance the experience, even reveal the design, in the limited dimensions available.

'I have chosen three five-word phrases. I want them to be simple, transportable, working like beacons to guide me home.'

The human being he was soon to become would have raised an eyebrow at this. He continued.

'They need to be truths, as I know they'll be competing with the loudest voice in my head, which will be the lies I tell myself.'

Simple statements projected with love. 'Is this useful to me?' 'Whatever I focus upon expands.' 'Is this who I am?'

'There will be other clues too,' the voice said.

'I know, I know, but it will be these that guide me home.'

'Take this with you,' the voice said.

Before him was a pouch pregnant with shining discs, reflecting the fifty or so primary colours that were left of this place.

'What is it?'

'It's a form of currency,' said the voice, 'there are 1,120 of them, the number of universal perfection. As before, your mission is not to spend any, but to bring them all home.'

'I recognise them,' he said, 'did I bring them back before?'

'You brought back 793 of them.'

'Was that good?'

'You are forgetting already that there is no "good", just as there is no "judgement" or "wrong". It will very soon be time.'

'Did others take them from me when I was last there?'

'No one can take them from you, they are only yours to give away.'

'I will bring them back when I return.'

The voice said nothing. Of all the colours there was only yellow, cyan and magenta left.

Two people sat at the bar a little apart on stools which kept getting stuck in the frays of carpet. A few metres away from them, his foot resting on a tarnished chrome rail, sat a man. He sat with the peak of a baseball cap pulled low over his forehead.

The two men sitting a little way from this man in a cap were earnest in their conversation, each leaning towards their beer. One of them looked at his watch. It was 1.45 and he felt a little guilty about delaying his return back to work after lunch.

On this winter's day, they had queued for a while at an unseasonably busy pizza place, losing the last table to a couple before giving up and deciding on the drink both of them were unable to justify to themselves following a slack morning's work.

'So that's it,' his companion said digging into the Bombay Mix that sat sweating on the bar, 'you're just going to accept it?' His thin, pale face looked out over the bar in frustration. He would have recognised the man in the cap sitting near to them had he, like his friend, seen him before.

'No, that's not it. There is so much more to it than that. It's redundancy not a warrant for my execution. Besides both of us know how miserable it has been for months at that place. What if—'

'Oh no!' his friend interrupted him. 'You're not going to do the "everything is for the best" routine, are you? Hunger is for the best because the food would have killed me, being dumped is for the best because she had the clap, killing a pedestrian on a pelican crossing is for the best because the dead guy might otherwise have accidentally done in Mozart's great-great-great grandson, or something?'

His friend observed him, noticing he was becoming more resourceful in producing his arguments as the afternoon developed. In the queue to the pizza place he had advocated taking out the whole board by spiking their coffee with weed-killer. He sighed. Was it exhaustion, or could he simply not elevate himself to that degree of anger?

'I don't know,' he said. 'What if this is the chance to get off our backsides and do something different, something better?'

'With just five grand redundancy? Are you insane? We've both given them the last six years of our lives, we certainly shouldn't give them the satisfaction of just crawling away.'

He knew his friend had a point. They probably could squeeze an extra couple of thousand out of the company if they acted in unison. But these days his focus seemed elsewhere. It felt more comfortable there. Two years ago he would have listed 'getting angry' among his strengths, and this fire had probably won him promotion a couple of times. He was the angriest salesman, volcanically moving from active to erupting with ease. But the messages in his life had changed some of that. He had begun to realise that when he put his attention on something and used his energy to support the focus, that thing became more real.

Did he want his anger to grow, or could he choose another part of him? What was that he had heard? 'Hit your pause button. Decide. Who are you in all of this? You have to be careful when you think about something because that something is going to get bigger the more you think about it.' Where had *that* come from? Who had said it to him?

'Do you have any idea who you are and what you can be?' His memory of the words, but not the speaker, was still clear. He found himself now desperate to hear more. It was as if this was a moment in time in which he was going to share something huge with himself.

Agonisingly, his memory of the conversation paused. He felt like someone had ripped the last four pages out of a book he had been reading and hidden them. It was a key moment in his life, although he was, at the time, oblivious to it. How could he know that life was a pack of playing cards, and the pathological events that would change everything were as the aces, hidden within the deck. The clues he had left for himself would be revealed at those times, but sometimes he would have to go back to the hand he had dealt himself to find them hidden behind the twos and fives.

Words such as this had, for him, been like radiotherapy. They became part of his inner self and worked long after the event. The clues came together later.

Back in the bar, he could hear some internal voice telling him that this was an opportunity. Perhaps even one he had created for himself. He made the mistake of saying this out loud to his friend, who was already round the other side of the conversation waiting for him.

'What? What a bloody sell-out! What are you, holier-than-thou or simply holier than me? You were the one who led the revolt two years ago, who got the board talking to us by holding them in a scrotal grip. You were the one who got the whole bonus thing restructured.

'Hey, *you* were the one who, by doing that, probably got us to where we are today – with no jobs. And you just want to skulk off now? Just like that?'

And there it was. The truth. He had been that man, it was true; although it had never actually happened in the way anyone remembered. Not that he had discouraged the legend and the telling of it over the last twenty-four months. He had been their champion at a time when they called out for one.

There was no question that man had been him. He had woken up with that man every morning ever since. He had shaved that man, showered him, fed him and had eaten cold curry out of tin trays straight from the fridge with him.

That man was a version of this man now sitting in a dingy bar, half watching the sunlight play with the optics in front of them. And why couldn't he change? he thought. Why couldn't he become another, better version of that man?

Did he know who he was and who he could be?

In the uncomfortable moment between them he did what men did; he started fiddling with his car keys. He turned the fob over in his hand as his friend glared at him over the bottle he was drinking from. He saw the word on the fob: 'Focus'. He would have to give that back, too. And the laptop. But, come on, he thought, a small Ford with a CD interchanger that was costing him an extra twelve pounds a month for every month he couldn't be fagged to go into the boot and change the CDs. So what?

As he played with the fob the sunlight shimmied around the display of bottles in front of them, bouncing off the glasses on the bar and finally catching the word enamelled on the key ring. That word shone. *Focus*. He knew he needed to fix his attention on a greater place. He would then use his energy to make that place more real.

This time he did not make the mistake of saying it out loud. Instead he said, 'You are right. We do deserve more than this. We have to decide, though, if it is they who are going to give it to us, or we who give it to ourselves. They are gits and they will always be gits. Making a fist of this just makes them gits who are defending themselves against fist-waving.'

His companion shook his head as if he was hearing the last rites being read to him. He looked defeated, as if the man before him was his power source and he was feeling it ebb away.

'Hang on,' he continued, 'what if we get smart about this? What if we focus our energy on that which is useful to the things we most want?' He picked up the key fob, examining it as if for inspiration.

'What is useful to us?'

'An extra two grand,' his friend replied hopefully.

'OK, an extra two grand is useful. Now let me ask you a different question. Using our nous, how do we best behave to make this situation work for us and so get that extra two grand?'

His friend shook his head as if to reorder the words so they could make sense.

'We go in there this afternoon and threaten to take everyone out unless they give us what we want,' he said.

'Right. Now you are the board. Your space is stormed by two people, who have just been made redundant and both of whom have a little, er, history. They push you into a corner, threaten you and then dish your last chance of dignity by bludgeoning the business that gives you your title, your kudos, your cash and your future. How do you feel and what do you do?'

'I don't care how they sodding well feel.'

There was the briefest pause for breath, so he took advantage of it.

'But you do care what they *do*, don't you?'

'What?'

'Well you care that they give you an extra two grand, don't you?'

There was a nod from behind the bottle.

'So we need to refocus. We need to care about how they feel in order to get what we want. It's easy, isn't it? If they lose it, we lose it. Except that our "it" is an extra two grand, possibly together with the original five grand.'

For him, though, in this exploration of himself, it wasn't about an extra two grand. That would be spent soon enough, and he would simply be the same angry bloke who had spent two grand more than he previously had.

He thought of the pause button; he thought of the way he was focusing his attention on other choices. He felt he was getting closer to who and what he could be, and that someone was handing him one of the four missing final pages from the end of the book. Part of him was struggling with this, as if wanting to shake off the calm he was feeling and go at it shoulder to shoulder with his friend. Part of him wanted to be the champion again.

That part of him was nagging away at himself. What if all of this is just claptrap? All this talk of 'choices' is just playing into their hands. It makes us weaker than them, so makes them more likely to win. Asking yourself 'Is this useful to me?' is a symptom of an erosion of your fighting spirit. It is a separation from what really matters on this planet – the constant battle to be heard above all the other voices that clamoured and shouted.

But another part of him wasn't struggling with it. This part knew that he was closer to a personal truth. Never having been here before, having always played the angry card first and second, he barely recognised himself. That part of him felt very peaceful and maintained its quiet inner voice that asked him, 'Is this useful to you?'

He knew this voice was his, but he didn't completely recognise it. This wasn't just about an extra two grand, this was about him. The choices he was making and the reasons he was making them. Why would he spend his creativity and resources on things that were not useful to him when he could directly attach his energy to better results?

His friend went to the gents, allowing him time to look around this ordinary bar. The man in the baseball cap just along the bar from them had been joined by a miserable looking man with ginger hair sticking up from his scalp like gelled stalactites. The ginger man appeared to be holding court on something. The tables were clearing now as people repaired back to their jobs; lunchtime was over. The man and the woman were left at one table. For some reason they seemed to be an odd couple; probably not a couple at all.

He noticed that she wore a really striking blue brooch, and as he looked at it...

'Give me a clue.' His train of thought was interrupted.

'What?' He turned round to see his friend return from the gents and launch himself into the dregs of the Bombay Mix on the counter.

'Give me a clue as to how we are going to approach this,' his friend said.

OK, he thought, let's really try this. 'Tell you what. I'll ask you a whole load of different questions and you just tell me whatever comes into your head. But remember, you have to answer as if everything has to be useful to whatever objective we decide upon.'

'What?'

'Well, let's decide, for the purposes of this exercise, that we are better than just a claim for more money; that this conversation actually represents what we most believe in.'

'You mean like "higher truths" and stuff like that?' The other man was kidding him, jostling to get a foothold in this conversation.

'OK, let's run with that for now. So, this becomes not entirely about the extra two grand but about our dignity, who we truly are.' He saw that he was losing his companion. The other man's face had moved from a semblance of openness to the beginnings of a frown. He went for the save. 'But the two grand is a huge part of our objective. It will be a sign that we are getting through... *one* of the signs.

'Every time we wander away from any of this we push our pause buttons. This will give us the chance to check if where we are is leading to where we want to be. Are you with me?'

The other man nodded. Nothing tangible had changed in his life. He still wanted an extra two grand, revenge and a chance to shout about how unhappy he was. But an unconscious part of him saw an ace poke out behind a nine in the hand of cards he was holding. That part of him, in search of clues, decided to listen rather than shout. The shouting part of him was surprised by the listener, had no idea about the clues and wouldn't have recognised them had he woken up beside them, naked.

The listening him didn't know about the clues either, had not yet met the man in the cap and would have claimed he had no pouch of shining discs.

The shouting him would have called the notion 'fucking bonkers', the listening him 'nonsense' and it would take a book of poetry left on the train and read out of distracted boredom to deliver the first real clue he has left himself.

Neither the shouter nor listener had ever read poetry before, so now he designed a situation where he would write his own. Not yet and not for a while; the spring was not yet here.

A couple of months later, this man, who thought that all poetry was 'pretentious bollocks' would allow his nascent instinct to send him up a path on a local hill overlooking the town that was causing him so much grief, to a small crumbling hut, its walls bursting with hardy and determined buddleia. There he picked up clues of his own; clues he had left there. Two days later he returned with a pad of paper and a pen to write the first poetry of his life. It was poetry he never dreamed he would write.

The awakening was a part of him that had seen golden embers of sunlight rippling on still water reflecting the last pair of egrets to take flight on a light evening breeze. It had gazed up at a round moon behind scuttling clouds watching over him as he walked over a thousand trillion grains of sand wrapped in a momentary blanket of peace.

This part hadn't known at the time that he was experiencing clues, but realised what he was feeling was about much more than he was seeing. It spoke to him in a voice so low and small as not to be heard and told him that he was to be a poet.

He might have been forgiven for thinking his poetry was for himself, or possibly for the man in the cap he would meet again in the spring, or his friend with the Ford Focus. How could he ever know it was written as a clue for another man who had designed it for himself?

It was another day three months later. The man in the bar had given back the Focus and the laptop, but felt that much richer for the lack of them. Part of him felt that for every year he aged he developed half a decade. And part of him just felt older.

If he had known that today was to be the freeze-frame snap-shot in his life he would have dressed better. Instead he was just kitted out for an errand.

He felt again for the pliant rustle of the bag in his left hand. Curling his fingers around the top of it, he wound the plastic up until he could feel the edges of its contents against his knuckles.

Standing for a while outside a travel agency it was a little time before he became conscious of playing the habitual game of wondering where he would rather be. The destinations were just words on pieces of jolly yellow card that urged pale people to 'brown themselves in the sun', miserable people to 'join the happy throng in Ibiza' and those who had spent a hopeful deposit on food and life to 'pay absolutely nothing until June'.

He had taken in three pictures of what appeared to be the same beach photographed at different angles and claimed to be of Mauritius, Fiji and 'your place in paradise' before he checked his thoughts. *This* was where he was. Was it 'want' and 'wish' and 'hope' that needed to expand in the world he was constructing? Making the mental correction that was getting easier and more natural he chose to focus his attention on this place, this life; this now. As in the bar three months before, he edged closer to a recognition that his internal language could actually make alterations to what he and about 7 billion others knew to be 'reality'. However, the more he attempted to attach his thoughts to it the fuzzier it got.

As he stepped closer to the periphery of what would undoubt-edly be regarded by some as insanity he had never felt more rational. But it was possible this was simply the final symptom of madness.

His head was full of questions. The questions were different to those that had orbited his mind a year ago, and he was deter-mined to make these different to those in the future that would circle his consciousness like summer flies.

'Holiday of a lifetime!' a larger and more orange card exhorted. A woman moved into a position to his right, her eyes like searchlights strafing the contents of the window for bargains and, just possibly, the trip that would turn her life around. She played a game with herself on her route to the bank, weighed down by the bar's cash takings. Quite why her boss trusted a cleaner to do the banking, she couldn't imagine; but it took her and her fantasies out on the road.

The rules of the game were simple. She would multiply today's date by the first number she saw when walking along the street. It was the 20th today, and there was an amazing looking silver car parked up by the baker's at the near end of the street with the registration number ABJ 56. She always could multiply numbers in her head. 'Gifted', her teacher had called her. 'Gifted'... She could multiply 56 and 20 in her head, but only afford meat for tea two nights a week. The total number was her budget as she window shopped her way out of the gloom of her everyday existence.

She would then cross her fingers, wish hard for the selected holiday and buy a scratch card at the newsagent's on the corner.

So far she had won two pounds and a free scratch card. Her friends from bingo told her that they liked how she never gave up hope. This wasn't true. She gave up hope every time she slipped her feet into old shoes, or forced a warped back door closed against the damp smell of her kitchen. But she still played the game with the yellow cards in the window. Silly, really. She felt that if she stopped playing the game she would have no hope left. And she needed that hope; it sustained her.

She became aware of a man standing next to her at the window, looking at her. It felt odd. She shuffled away to buy a scratch card. The holiday for two for ten days on St Kitts came in at just under today's fantasy cumulative amount. She linked this place to the latest postcard from her son. It would be so good to see him again. Could this be a sign? Did she believe in signs? She wished, she hoped, she wanted to win. Maybe she would treat herself to two scratch cards and drink tap water at lunchtime. Sometimes, there were half sandwiches left over behind the bar and those smelly peanuts, like feet, with crunchy bits and hot raisins. Two scratch cards and another free lunch could be all she needed.

The man with the bag watched the woman move away from where they had been standing together. He had the feeling that neither of them had been searching for their annual holiday in this window of hope.

He touched the top of the bag again. There was no way he could put this off anymore. Three weeks before he had bought the object that lay in the bottom of the bag, taunting him with its defective uselessness. '*Why?*' his wife had asked him. It was obviously a 'man thing'. To him, the fact that it had a plug, a string of coloured lights and an LCD counter was reason enough. Did you have to be a man to get this? Other men got it in the way that women got shoes and Johnny Depp.

His attempted explanation hadn't satisfied her in the slightest. It cost twenty-nine ninety-nine, she had persisted, the alliterative words betraying her German heritage. He had shown her how it worked and stood back from it in the same way as men do when showing someone a spanner set. '*Look!*' his body language had yelled. '*Now* do you get it?'

She had looked at it and back to him, her mystification filling the space between them. Why could she not see it, and why (now he had started) when she refused to order a pudding of her own did she insist upon spooning his? 'Why not just *order* one?' he always pleaded.

'I told you I don't want one,' she always replied, even as she carefully excavated another spoonful away from the area of dessert he had not touched.

He was convinced that this was a species, not a gender issue. And since the damn bloke thing with lights and a plug had stopped working, the chasm had grown. She had caught him pacing around it with a screwdriver.

'If you take it apart you cannot take it back to the shop.'

'It might just need, you know, tweaking,' he said, waggling the screwdriver at it.

'Do you have the receipt?'

'I think your hairdryer might have magnetised it.'

'Do you know at all what you are talking about?' Apparently she was not to be deflected.

He had tried to look despairing. The word 'magnetised' had been his long shot.

'I mended the TV, didn't I?'

'No, you destroyed it. We had to get a man in, don't you remember?'

A man in? What was this? Wasn't he a man, and wasn't he 'in'?

'Do you have the receipt?' she persisted.

No, and he didn't have the box or the bag it had come in, either. The bag in his left hand was of a similar colour to the main part of the logo of the shop to which he was now returning it. He stood outside the shop as if examining the displays that were arranged to lure him in. Two flickering screens surrounded by lots of smaller ones in the window ogled him as if knowing his present weaknesses and future intentions.

As he stood there examining other intriguing things with flashing lights and digital readouts he constructed his arguments. He hated this. He hadn't kept the receipt. But come on, who did? Who kept all of their receipts, and what kind of lives did these people live? As he rehearsed in front of his reflection in the window, the conversation he was yet to have took root and started to grow. His mind fashioned the perfect lies, spiralling arguments and counter-arguments, raised voices, accusations and denials. The enemy in the shop would fight their corner, deny that the model was sold there, look at it as if he had dropped it in a bucket of cockles, quote their rules at him and force him to leave defeated, some other shop's bag in his hand.

He would then return home, humiliated, to explain all of this to his foot-tapping wife, his ignominy and shame doubling in the retelling; the Germanic ranging of arguments perfectly constructed against him.

All of this he knew before he went in to the shop. He could taste it, smell it, and the resonance of the arguments bounced about his head like tombola balls in a barrel. But he had no choice, and finally stepped across the threshold and into the fray.

If only the internal arguments had resonated less loudly, he might have heard five other words playing in his mind.

'Whatever you focus upon expands.'

He approached the counter. It was as if the shop assistant had read the script of his life. She seemed to stand there waiting for him. She was a strange, amorphous being, gothically cloaked in layers of black. Her tarmac eyeliner acted like a staple at each eye's corner, narrowing them as if in constant suspicion. Neither of her eyes focused on him, nor anything else as he resolutely strode towards her domain. The nearer he got, the more gold blobs and circles he could see protruding from her face, two of them standing out against the black of her lips.

He looked down at her badge as if to bolster himself. 'Trainee' it assured him. He dumped the bag on the counter, its contents clunked against the glass.

'I want to bring this back,' he said a little too loudly.

Her eyes moved a little, but neither in the direction of him nor the bag. They just shifted. Did he see an inner eyelid blink briefly across them?

She said nothing.

This is *precisely* what his imagination had concocted. Defensiveness, aggression, he could feel it surround him, suffocating his rationality, his very humanity, as he stood there pressed against the counter. People in the shop, back out in the street, even those passing in their unimportant little hatchbacks were looking at him and his wrong logo bag. He was pulling a fast one, they thought, trying it on. They could see the scratched plastic where he had assaulted it with a screwdriver, knew he hadn't kept the receipt and were whispering their questions about where he had really bought it, and when. They hadn't sold that range for over a year now. They couldn't ever remember carrying that model. It wasn't one of theirs. It couldn't be. Theirs never went wrong. And even if they had sold one like that, no one had ever returned one of those and they had sold them for more than 1200 years. Had anyone witnessed him allegedly buying it, and would they be prepared to swear to that in a court of law?

'I'm not taking no for an answer.' An angry pilot in his head had called 'rotate' seconds before. He was at take-off velocity; there was no going back now. He took the defunct, pointless bloke thing out of the bag and banged it on the glass counter.

This clanging noise, and the elevation of his tone, caused the head of the amorphous gothic creature to bob. It was a curious feral reaction, allowing great swathes of black hair that had previously flooded either side of a white face to fall in front of her eyes. Rather than push it back she started to shake her head in an alarming way, as if tossing a mane of crows from the front of her face. The girl may have hissed the word 'exchange' as she studiously avoided all eye contact, or maybe she just sighed.

'I don't want to exchange it, I want my money back. *Now.*' His voice was raised, his fight mechanism activating.

Something sparked in the gothic creature. The extensive training she had received this morning, the first day of her first part-time job, as she walked in from the bus stop, with an assistant associate fellow trainee, kicked in. The crows settled briefly as she took a breath.

'Do you have the receipt?' She asked in a much smaller voice than her image suggested.

Well, that was it, wasn't it? he thought. The wholly expected assault on his manhood, his value system, his trustworthiness and everything he stood for. He launched his attack. The first volley of shock and awe.

'No, I don't have the bloody receipt, Jeez, no, of *course not*! Are you calling me a liar? Who the *hell* do you think you are? *Who keeps receipts, for God's sake?*'

He violently shook the wrong-logo bag onto the counter as if in emphasis as he railed at this assault. Ironically, a receipt for another item from another shop floated out of it and settled gently on the counter between them. For a split second they watched together as it lay on the glass top.

'Is this what you call customer service?' he yelled. The under-carriage was up and the runway was fast disappearing behind the pilot in his head. 'You should be ashamed!'

There was something else, the gothic creature thought. Something she should say. A very small part of her mind searched for it among the debris that was flying around in the whirlwind of this assault. What was it that was written on the notice board beside the empty water butt in the stinking kitchen next-door to the loo?

It's company policy, she remembered suddenly. She decided to say it.

'What?' He screamed back at her. 'What?'

'P-p-policy,' she stammered.

He swore at her, loud and hard. He didn't hold back. He

didn't care if it was useful to him. He swore again. She recoiled as he shouted, her head bobbing furiously, the mane of crows all taking to the sky together squawking and calling in a mass of black.

'Do you have a pet I can talk to?' he shouted. The plot had been lost too long before, it wasn't a question of customer service or what was right. This was a matter of survival, of life and death, to the part of him that couldn't believe he was having this conversation.

The gothic creature slowly turned and walked away from the counter. She remembered there was a door into the back of the shop. There would be help there and her attacker couldn't follow. He watched her go and swung his gaze around the shop as if searching for other targets.

Thirty-eight years, two months and eleven days later he died.

The first thing that tipped him off was the buzzing noise. It wasn't a noise he could hear, as much as feel. He was aware in a vague, unconcerned way, of a number of people running around, looking very busy with cumbersome looking metal objects, some of them on wheels.

There was no time left. He heard one of the people call out, 'He's gone,' in an anxious tone, and was aware of looking around to check who was missing. No one was there. No one was anywhere.

He was surrounded by the deepest of blacks. It was not so much a void as a shape. Funnel-shaped. The area immediately around him was misty grey, but it was in every way inconsequential as there was no solidity anymore. He realised that now he was no longer physical density, but waves, patterns, like a ball of energy.

The funnel was very narrow and he was not aware he was moving at all until he saw the globe of light. It was rushing towards him at an inconceivable velocity. He had no words for any of this; adjectives were like blades of grass against an advancing army. This was what the buzzing noise was, the absence of language. And yet there was only peace. Unbelievable peace. It was as if there could be and never was anything else.

As the light grew he became aware of moving through and past things around him. He saw someone he knew to be the neighbour of his parents who had fallen into a thresher when he was eleven, at least one grandparent, his history teacher, a bicycle and the Labrador they had mourned more than sixty years ago. He wanted to think, Thumper? How does *that* work? but had no time. There was no time.

In a cartoon moment of suddenness the funnel and the globe combined and light was all there was. But it was not light, because there was no place where darkness began, and because it was part of his sight, not something he was seeing. And then it was not light. It was a being. A being that emanated a sense of inestimable ease.

'Hello,' the being said.

How could he explain to himself that there was no 'saying', in the same way that there was no 'doing', 'talking' or 'explaining'?

'Welcome back,' the being added.

He was part of something else now. The something else had no edges or boundaries, which was handy because neither did he. There were also a staggering number of colours everywhere, morphing with sounds that he found himself utterly besotted with. He and the being moved around this feeling as if by will, arriving in a place that could have been a room, or just another level of feeling.

There had to be some sense somewhere.

'Is this heaven?' he asked. The being looked at him as if he might be thinking, Oh, dear Lord, a Christian. The sounds and light in the room combined to be a chair and he placed his non-physical but completely recognisable self into it. He had to admit, he thought to what was no longer himself, the soft furnishings in heaven were pretty comfortable.

Before them a screen-type image appeared, sliding down from what could have been, at a push, described as the ceiling. In fact it was more like an extension of what they were feeling together.

The light in the room dimmed perfectly and the chair he was placed in slid towards it. He suddenly had an idea that belonged somewhere else.

'Is this judgement?' he asked.

The being might have looked now as if he was thinking, another Jew, Muslim, Hindu… but instead just said, 'Watch.'

Together they watched something appear on the screen in omni-dimensions. It enveloped them into a place which he recognised as one scene from his life. The scene had taken place thirty-eight years, two months and eleven days before.

He saw himself outside the shop with a bag in his hand. He saw his thoughts stretching out from him, constructing what was to happen when he walked in. He felt and heard, as well as saw, his own despair, frustration, aggression, defensiveness as he watched himself stride into the shop.

He saw himself from behind the eyes of every person around him and, for the first time, saw a beautiful young girl swathed in make-up, raven hair and layers of black. The assistant behind the counter. He watched himself slam the bag down onto the glass. He heard what he said and felt everyone else's reactions to it.

He saw every second of the conversation a hundred times in the space of a single moment and finally, after quite literally no time at all, he heard him shout at the top of his voice.

'Do you have a pet I can talk to?'

He saw the girl disappear from the counter and retreat through the door at the back of the shop. Then he saw what he had not seen when he was alive. He saw her cry. He saw a small, perfect, hopeful, wonderful girl cry. He saw her tears pour down white cheeks like channels of mud, carrying mascara and the hopes for her first day in her first job with them.

And as he saw this the light returned, the screen disappeared and his chair slid back to join the being who had watched everything with him. He felt it all at once as they reconnected. The remnants of who he had been were still around him and he thought to himself, am I damned?

The being surrounded him. There was no sense of accusation or judgement. He joined the thoughts of the being as they combined. He heard, felt and experienced the reaction to his own thought. Damned? How could you be? Where do you think you are? Then he heard the being think, no, I only have one question.

'Is that who you were?'

He disconnected and looked back at the being. Suddenly the

adjectives and adverbs filled him as they had in his life on the planet at the other end of the funnel.

'That's hardly fair,' he said, 'you cannot just pick one fleeting moment from seventy-eight years on a material, exacting, difficult planet and play it back to me as if it represented everything I was, or felt, or did.

'I had three children, I loved them, I saved a man's life when I was thirty-two, I wrote books, trained people to respect themselves and others, created laughter and listened to people when they needed it, I was loved, I...'

The words that had returned to him began to fail, and all the time the being looked at him, totally at ease and without a sense of appraisal or assessment. When he was finished, when all of the words were over, the being connected with him again and the words came to him.

'But how did you know?'

'What?' he said.

'How did you know that this moment, this event, wasn't the reason you were on that planet? How did you know that everything else was not either leading up to it, or away from it? How could you take that risk? What did you base it on? Why should it be "the children" or "the wisdom" or "the books" or "the job"? How did you know?'

'I didn't know, I couldn't know,' he said.

'No,' said the being.

The room and anything else that felt like separation had almost disappeared. The being had also become a part of him, and was now a voice.

'Did you bring anything back?' the voice asked him.

Together they looked to where fingers had been. There was a pouch still pregnant with shining discs.

'There are 1,019 discs. You did incredibly well,' the voice said.

Of the 1,120 discs he had taken with him one hundred and one had been spent. Now he remembered. He remembered everything. He knew that the discs were like energy. Choices. When he had made a decision to spend his energy in a way that served who he truly was, the discs remained in their pouch. When he made a choice that did *not* reflect the true experience of being alive on the planet, he effectively chose to remove a disc from the pouch.

That day in the shop he had removed a disc from the pouch.

Now he was back there was no judgement and no disappointment. There was only experience.

'I need to go back,' he said.

'Need?' queried the voice.

'I *choose* to go back,' he corrected himself. He had not yet unlearnt the habits of his most recent trip.

He continued. 'To have the experience of life on that planet and return with all of the discs is what we all do.'

'To return with 1,019 is perfect too, you realise. To return with one would be to experience other things, and there is perfection in every part of that.'

Yes,' he persisted, 'but what must I do to return with all 1,120?'

'Maybe you need to send yourself better clues.'

Somewhere back on the planet someone picked up a lost purse on a train and walked two miles under a perfect moon to return it to its worried owner. Somewhere else on the same planet a woman sat by the side of a lake watching herons dive for fish. She looked up and saw what could have been her name etched in the clouds before they scuttled off to hug the tailfin of a passing aircraft. Somewhere else, an envelope containing a bright blue brooch fell through the letterbox of a woman cloaked in sadness. What had she just sent herself?

Better clues…

The Designer

At some point the undulating lines of green gave way to the suburbs. It had been a record-breaking April; too much rain had fallen from the isobars and too little sun had warmed the new buds lately unfolded against a shivering spring. Patchwork fields crept up to small copses of oak and birch trees, pushing up their crops of rape, wheat and beet, to greet the first day of warmth after a long winter.

Early lambs had grown big enough to graze away from exhausted mothers on the edges of a field close to the town, having gained the confidence to stray, and look forward to a future of rosemary and mint.

A late train squealed along steel lines outlining the fringe of the countryside, and none of the four horses shaking their heads in the pasture separated from the lambs by hedges of golden bell forsythia and gorse looked up to wonder at this whine of humanity.

The depth and variety of greens that made up the town's borders was almost shocking in its vibrancy. Pea, bottle, forest, lime, olive and loden all threw their best against the palette of the landscape. Wave upon wave of horse chestnut and smooth-leaved elm seemed to rush up to the outskirts as if eager to show off the florets of a new season. Cylindrical and round, white and pink, they proudly presented the trophies of a new spring. White willows, their branches bent to the ground again by new leaves shining silver in the light, still heavy with catkins. All of these joined fresh bronze cones of grand firs with pale fingers of new growth pointing upwards at the blue of a sky that provided a perfect backdrop to what could have been a celebration of the first day of the world.

From this sky could be seen the ginger bouncing dot of a red setter launching itself in and out of the tall grasses of a field laid fallow. The dog stopped briefly to sniff the stew of smells that made up the casserole of early summer, snapping at flies and catching a glimpse of his tail that suddenly seemed remarkable to him. He was momentarily distracted by the head of a mare appearing over a low point in the hedge to pull at a twig of leaves made tempting by the fact it was in a field other than hers. The setter gave a bark – part joy, part surprise – before spotting something more compelling on the other side of his field and bounding off to investigate.

The whining train, still at odds with the rigour of its timetable, hurled itself at a hole in the countryside, disappearing under a tall mound thick with hawthorns. A path wound up this hill, dived into the thicket and emerged on the other side to think better of its journey and slink off down again. On the rim of this dense wood stood a small crumbling hut, its walls bursting with hardy and determined buddleia. In this hut a man sat looking out over the landscape and made up poetry he thought he would never share.

The poet had the thin, pale face and long fingers of an artist, but the troubled mind of the masses. A distant part of his nascent instinct had sent him up this hill to be alone with thoughts plagued by doubt.

His defences had been breached by the catastrophic failure of confidence caused by a pincer movement on his life by the twin armies of redundancy and depression. His discovery of the hut with its view back over the town that had failed him granted sanctuary. It gave him the space to think, and his thoughts led to words that spawned wisdom he considered no one would ever need.

When he wrote down his thoughts he started simply. If there was a point to everything, it wasn't this; a man-made carousel of dashed hopes and false starts. Yet his instinct demanded to be heard on this hill. The emerging poet initially saw only the bleakness of a town feeding off the natural wonder around it. As he looked further he spotted individual clues in the perfection around him, cowering like lone SuDoku numbers in the nine-by-nine grid of life. As the words came, the poet saw the numbers too, and started to add new ones as his eyes opened wider before the sublimity of it all. It was then he started to write.

Some of this poetry described his wonder at what surrounded him: the spires of Lombardy poplar and incense cedar trees congregating with churches to make exclamation marks at the end of wooded sentences, sometimes encircled by strands of early morning mist and hawks searching for their breakfast; slashes of brown roofs and brick walls unexpectedly revealed between the trees; a still convoy of yellow trucks and diggers sleeping in a lay-by waiting for the day to begin. An abandoned Gothic water tower with an entourage of elders at its base erected imperiously on a distant hill peered out towards orchards of newly planted hybrid larch trees lined up like soldiers, holding their ground and awaiting the commands of their red oak generals on the side of roads.

During his days of healing up on the hill, the reluctant poet had watched the town edge closer. Green became brown as the diggers moved in. Brown turned into rows of grey as concrete foundations, like catacombs, were laid. Finally, shoots of bricks emerged from the ground which quickly grew to embrace tiny rooms where the dreams of their new occupiers would eventually hatch.

Thin splinters of garden were roughly turfed by builders to await the pots and neatly planted borders of their owners, who would invite nano-parts of the country back into its former domain. The new householders would drive across the fields on narrow winding roads to garden centres, cursing the inconvenience of this rural beauty, before returning home to install a pale reflection of it on their patios.

On this warm spring day, the frayed borderlines of the countryside waved their fronds at yet another housing development standing resolute behind a wall so big, fine and perfect that it took on a cartoon-like quality. If Berliners had seen this wall they would have made a mental note to take pickaxes to it in fifty years. If the poet had seen it from his hut he would have drawn gargoyles and parapets into its description. Yet one day he would see a woman sitting on a wall close to the boundary of this incipient cityscape and witness her fashion an escape. That night he even dreamed of showing her his words before watching her walk away.

But for now, behind the wall, houses lined up like brickwork brush strokes framing the paint-by-numbers lives of those who lived within its boundaries.

People resided in symmetrical lines living parallel lives, timing themselves by the habits of others in a place where wrist muscles were made strong by the twitching of curtains. The Neighbourhood Watch scheme had no need for criminals, and identical roads which defined the parameters of each area soon fostered resentment and competition. When Number 53 on one road bought a new shape Mondeo, it was a relief to Numbers 37 to 89 on another when Number 36 then bought one.

When the daughter of 'that couple over the shop' fell pregnant at the age of fourteen, the indignity and incomprehension of the couple who ran the video store were magnified by the fact that theirs had held out until she was at least sixteen.

From any passing aircraft, drawing vaporised signatures in the sky, the rows of houses blurred together. Indistinguishable, inseparable. The word for this conurbation had not grown up from the Latin for 'population together', but from the need to excuse and explain a graveyard of humanity.

From the ground, the size of conservatory and extension over the garage was a statement of manhood. The people at Number 73 went without a holiday to relay their drive with herringboned bricks when those two roads down on the corner put down gravel. Yet they laughed together one Christmas when sharing stories about their common enemy, the lawyer on Acacia, who had a two-berth caravan in his drive.

'It's *so* yesterday,' the man from 73 said, smiling behind his hand.

'I'm not sure it was even then,' came the giggled rejoinder, presumably forgetting they had in-laws with a static on the coast.

From above it all, high on his hill overlooking the town, the poet watched. There was a growing sense of anticipation about the day. He felt a slight breathlessness he had come to recognise as a sign of connection with something greater. He once described this in one of his poems as the ring of a telephone just prior to contact.

He couldn't see or hear anyone within the expanding grid of

life spread out beneath him, but knew he was part of them. He felt the slight stutter and instant kick-start of a missed heartbeat as he thought about the two days to come. He had taken a leap and decided to spend some of the exit currency from his redundancy package on a training course which threatened to 'Design Your Future Life'. But a growing part of him knew this alone was not the reason for the thrill he felt ripple through his body.

He looked towards the buildings ranging into the distance below him; somewhere in there that reason was waking up to the new day.

Today the houses had emptied into cars and onto trains and buses between seven thirty and nine o'clock. Two identical blue cars reversed out of similar driveways three roads apart but no more than 300 metres and thirty seconds away from each other, inadvertently partnering each other in the daily dance of the commute. Their drivers had no conscious memory of ever having seen one another, despite the fact that they had designed strikingly comparable lives for themselves. They worked in the same job for different companies, both of whom marketed themselves as being 'remarkable'. They both liked Thai food and were thinking of taking up golf (although neither ever would). They had both married their childhood sweetheart, but each secretly fantasised about the women on the paint counter at the hardware store on the bypass. Neither of them believed in God, but they would simultaneously realise they had totally missed the point at the crack of an amazing dawn fourteen years later.

In a neighbouring house a woman who had once believed in a wholly different God stood staring out of her kitchen window, up to her elbows in suds, drowning in desperation. She looked across the road at the blank windows of a replica house and thought she could see herself stare back out of the darkness. She wiped her forehead with the back of her hand, leaving stray bubbles on the end of her nose which she blew off onto the glass of the window in front of her. She watched as a streak of soapy water played its way down to the ledge below where two plants wilted, resolutely dying, their leaves turning brown at the edges.

She looked at a cup with a chipped rim standing on the drainer by the sink. Has it really come to this? she thought.

She instantly recognised this inauthentic thought as one heard on a television soap opera the evening before. The context of the sentiment had been different on this show, the person saying it having discovered that her sister had been sleeping with her husband and was now carrying twins, which she herself was incapable of conceiving, and who could only be saved by a life-threatening blood transfusion that only she could give.

'Has it really come to *this*?' the character had screamed, the climax of a tortured row about infidelity and betrayal.

Making this connection, she now thought ruefully, so not about a cup, then. But then she realised that for her it wasn't about a cup, either.

She had the dream again last night. The long, dark hole that both felt and smelt dank enveloping her, sucking her in. This time it had been a little different. For the first time she didn't plunge endlessly into the hole, but returned to the surface, and when she awoke, gasping for breath as she always did, saw a smudge of dawn curling around the top of the curtains.

Thinking about this now she glanced at the picture of the little girl, smiling back at her as she always did from behind the non-reflective glass that held her frozen in time.

She remembered being the same age as that little girl. Her life had been riddled with the cancer of fear of death. She would wake up screaming in the night, flanked by her anxious parents, choking with fear, imagining each breath would be her last and that she would be sent plunging down the same dark hole that plagued the dreams she still had as an adult and a mother. Her parents would tell her that it was all right, that she was safe, but her little mind knew better. She had felt what death could do; it called her, and she knew that one day she would not be able to resist and that all the love in the world would not enable her parents to hold on to her as she sank down through the bed, into the hole and away from them.

She recalled being separate from the other children who played bit parts in her young life. 'Serious and intense', her teachers called her in school reports. She remembered looking up the word 'intense' in the dictionary when she read it. She didn't know if she was being criticised, and it forced her deeper into herself. She chose to be a lawyer because it meant she could find an excuse for long hours of study, with no time to socialise with people around her. And when she met her husband and they decided to have children she felt that, at last, some part of her could be released; it would fly from the sentence of death revealed in the dreams that never left her.

Five doors down and two across from this mentally exhausted lawyer was the almost identical house of a man who had never met this woman, and who was sitting on a train in the same seat he had chosen to commute from for the past five years. He had seen the same TV soap opera last evening, and when the woman pregnant with her brother-in-law's children had been confronted by her sister, the denouement of many a nights' viewings, he had been in the kitchen licking coleslaw off his fingers. Having missed the line his near neighbour and distant stranger had just repeated to herself at her kitchen sink, he had rushed back into the room.

'What did she say?' he asked his wife, who was draped over files and papers on the table by the window. His wife looked at him over her reading glasses, as if searching in her memory for the name of a stranger.

'Hmm?'

'What did she say – the redhead? You know, the sister; what did she say?'

His wife glanced at the television set across the other side of the room. Something stirred, she had heard the shape of the words; she took a stab.

'He's done for Chris.' She returned to the invoices on the top of the pile in front of her.

'Chris? *Chris?* Who the hell is Chris?' her husband squeaked.

His wife dragged herself back to the conversation.

'Isn't he the guy who slept with the blonde one when her husband was fighting chemical fires in Iran?'

'No, *no!*' Her husband slapped his forehead, leaving spots of coleslaw sticking to his fringe. 'He was killed in a freak airship incident in the last series. And his name was Dish, not Chris.'

'Interesting,' his wife said. Where is that other memo? she thought.

None the wiser, and on the train the following morning this

man, a master commuter, found himself shivering without reason in an overwarm carriage whose heating had been taken by surprise on this first real day of spring. He was suddenly racked by a feeling from nowhere; from out of the blue it dominated the beautiful April sky. Just ten minutes away from the real start of a day that would have terrified a less resilient man, he recognised the symptoms of anxiety. What had caused this latest outbreak? Hadn't all of this been settled the day before? Not again, surely? Just as yesterday, with another packed schedule, this certainly wasn't the time or the day for it. He readied himself for a fight he recognised.

However, on this day the feeling appeared to be growing in intensity from a different source. He inwardly searched the local area of usual anxiety and found himself looking out of the window for solace, the unplaced distress growing within him. No, this wasn't the same at all. He searched his feelings; the child was away somewhere else, playing happily. So what was this?

Just as the feeling reached crisis point, a part of his subconscious reached out and united him with the tendrils of fear that connected him to another soul in the conurbation they shared. His conscious mind sought tangible affirmation of something it could not comprehend, and grasped at the sudden emergence out of the train window of a group of apartments braced around a basin of water: a conspicuous oasis in an industrial suburb. He found himself counting the apartment blocks as the train sped past. Twelve, eleven… two, one. The panic eased. He shook his shoulders and went back to his paper. Tuesday mornings, he thought, he could never get used to Tuesday mornings.

Seven rows down and five across from where this master commuter and his wife lived, facing a sorry patch of grass that, in an unhatched planning application, was supposed to 'resemble the squares and parks of Chelsea and Kensington', but in fact looked like an untended allotment, a woman left her house and checked each front door lock the customary four times before setting off in her usual way to the dry cleaners. She counted the gateposts to the corner and avoided the drain cover that she knew would move if she put any weight on it. She had seen others step on it, almost as if they were unaware of its dangers, and couldn't understand why they would take such a risk.

She tacked across seven roads, forming the first letter of each of their names into the mnemonic she had practised for the 1,120 days she had taken the identical journey: a memorised ginger-bread trail, in case of emergency. Five houses down on the left she looked up, as she always did, at the huge satellite dish on the front of the house of the couple she imagined must live there. Why would they have this monstrosity on the front of their house? What was the point? It was ghastly, unsightly, and all it did was to encourage more television of a nature that was wholly inappropriate.

Why couldn't it be put round the back where it couldn't be seen, or in the shed (a cheap one, quite dilapidated) she had always pictured to be at the bottom of the back garden of the house. Why not in the shed?

She sometimes wondered why this dish offended her so much. She never found out exactly why; she just knew it did and that it was the first negative sign she had to counter with a positive one now only three roads away. She knew a lot of things about the people she had never met whose lives surrounded but never touched hers. She could hear them laughing through closed doors, waiting for her to get lost. She occasionally saw them shirtless in their front yards surrounded by too many children, making as if not to see her but wondering about the life she kept safely locked away from them; plotting against her behind their hands, pretending to cough or wipe sweat from their upper lips.

But as long as she could count and remember, she knew she need never get lost and was convinced that, although she was later today, if she hurried and the blue car was still in the drive, this was an omen of safety. Of sanctuary. She knew she was later today. The telephone call from the silent stranger had delayed her by a few minutes. She rounded the corner and saw the blue car already making its way towards the end of the road. She started to panic. The bile of fear rushed up to her throat, her heart pounded. This and the dish were bad omens. She saw a woman packing suspicious packages into the boot of a little red car, checking the brooch she was wearing twice, three times. This was the third sign. She knew something. What could it be? Fear continued to sweep through her. There was only one thing it could mean. She knew that she hadn't properly locked her front door. Despite all those years of checking and being careful, she could see those men in her house, ransacking her drawers, finding the things she had hidden from them. Knowing about her life. A life she had kept from the prying eyes of everyone in this place.

She started to panic, looking wildly towards her route back, seeing two roads, three, leading away from her. *Keep calm*, she told herself. She had to keep calm. Poppleton, Winterburn, Stapleton.

Her mind whirled, the mist was descending. Poppleton, Winterburn, Stapleton… Wickham. What was next? What was after Wickham? Wickham, Trennon, *Napier* (or was it Morston?). Poppleton, Winterburn, Stapleton, Wickham, Trennon, Napier (no, it was definitely Napier). But she needed to know the last road. Her heart pounded, she could no longer see clearly. There were two leading off Napier, and only one of them led home. What if she turned the wrong way? What would happen? Her breath had become shallow and fast. She made herself slow down. Only that way could she think. People Weep Silently When The Night *Falls*. Falls. F… *Falstow*. It was Falstow. She could make it home.

She was panting now, but she knew the way home. Virtually running as she crossed Falstow, she knew she would see the green soon and would instantly be able to see that her front door had been forced open. She turned the last corner, careful even in her distress to step over the drain cover. Twelve gateposts and she would be home. Eleven; she could see her front door now. It looked closed. Everything might be all right. Two gateposts… one. She ran up her path and pushed on the door. It was closed. She tried the handle, it was locked.

She unlocked the two central locks and the one at the bottom. She was safe now, there was nothing to be afraid of. She went in.

The heartbeat of the estate that had quickened during this panic gradually slowed again. Its life was the people who lived there within its tarmacadam lines. It worked with them, laughed with them and loved with them. They were its soul, the creators of not only its complexity, but the simplicity of its purpose. On their own, furiously concentrating on living their lives, they were blissfully unaware of this. When they finally joined together they would know. The poet made his way down the hill, his heartbeat beginning to slow again. He checked his pocket once more for the directions of the course that would design his future life.

Outside the house with the line of suds streaking the kitchen window, the lawyer prepared to leave for the same training event. As she packed her bags into the back of her hatchback, she abruptly took a sharp intake of breath. Without warning she felt a wave of dizziness sweep over her. As she fought to ease her breathing she could feel her heart pounding against her chest. She slumped heavily against the car door. What was this? It was about ten years too early for the menopause and she searched her memory for any dubiously late eat-by dates from the ingredients of last night's meal. Nothing. It was weird. Then, as quickly as the feeling had swept over her, it had gone.

This incipient portent of doom confirmed something she already knew; this was one damn training opportunity she could do without. How many times could Human Resources enthusiastically tick a box on a personal development plan when someone clearly could not be developed? She didn't need it, didn't want it, couldn't take it; yet she did not have a fever and couldn't think of any reason not to attend. One fleeting 'female moment' against the door of a small red French car did not constitute a reasoned excuse.

She patted the collar of her jacket three times. On it was an ice blue brooch, almost exactly the colour of the memory of her mother's eyes. She could go nowhere without it. She had been devastated to lose it. For a while she couldn't even think about its loss, could barely breathe through the pain it caused. Then it had been returned to her in an unmarked envelope, pushed through her letter box. The strangeness of its return had almost outweighed the sense of its loss. But now she checked once again that it was securely fastened.

Moments earlier she had phoned a number she was convinced was that of Human Resources, and a woman had answered. She suddenly thought better of offering weak and pathetic excuses for her absence on the course to the girl who worked there with too many vowels at the end of her forename. Besides, the voice that answered sounded older, almost afraid, and she hit the 'end call' button rather than explain herself.

No, she had to go. The boys had said they would feed the cat, but she felt she would rather leave the cat in charge. For a second her heart missed another beat. Why did part of her feel desperate to get away from them? What was this constant need to keep moving, to run away? When would she stop? How could she ever stop? She knew that in the kitchen the little girl smiled at her from behind non-reflective glass, and she knew she never would.

She checked the bags were in the back of the car, returned to make sure she had not put the cat food timer back into the cupboard, examined herself for signs of a virus in the mirror by the front door, locked herself out and stood in her front yard.

She had the details of the course in her hand. It was only two days, it might even allow her to stop thinking.

'So what, you're telling me that life just happens? It's an accident. Stuff happens, stuff stops happening and then we all gently expire to make way for accidents happening to other pointless biological improbabilities?'

'It's better than all that crap about "meaning" and "destiny" and, you know, collective intelligence.' It was the first time he had decided to take on the man at the front of the room.

The trainer looked at him curiously. He had assumed a Christine Keeler posture on the chair placed in the opening of an incomplete circle of people. It was nearing the end of day one of the course. The walls were plastered with the summary of the topics covered so far. Over the shoulder of the delegate who had challenged his viewpoint, he could see one of four flip chart pages he had used to wallpaper the room prior to the delegates' arrival. It said, 'The only sin of mankind is to die with your music still in you.' He wondered how many of the people before him knew how to play their music.

The clock to his left said '4.35'. He felt the group was ready. In fact, he felt that if he pushed a skewer into two of three of them they would be running clear. If not now, when? If not these people, who?

'Better how, exactly?' he said.

A man with curiously fashioned facial hair looked back at him. It was a position he had taken before in bars all over the south-east. He didn't really know what he believed, but felt certain about what he didn't believe.

'So what, you buy all this "God stuff", do you?' he asked of the man in front of the group.

'What is so offensive to you about other people realising that they are greater than they previously thought? How does that affect you? Is your agnosticism so fragile?'

'It's just the way they bang their drums. The hallelujah set. It makes me sick. It's only their way, at their time, with their God.'

'What about the others?' The trainer cocked his head at the rest of the world.

'Others?'

'Yes, the others. The ones who do not bang drums. The ones who simply realise who they are, and therefore who they can be.'

A woman in the group with streaked blonde pigtails gave him the look she had practised a couple of times previously as together they had paced the boundaries of the training course.

'Who do *you* think they realise they are?' she asked of the trainer. It was a question that seemed to have the permission of her colleagues.

The atmosphere in the room changed almost imperceptibly. In a synchronous stutter the air conditioning fan clicked off then on again instantaneously. The flip chart paper on the stand fluttered slightly, then fell still. The bearded man started to play with the laces on his trainers.

'They are the designer,' came the response. The trainer wondered briefly what impact this may have.

He knew that some of them wanted to ask and wondered what their barrier to asking was. The questioner with the pigtails didn't want to ask. She was comfortable with the silence that preceded understanding. The bearded man felt that he had sidelined himself from the 'wanting to ask' group with his previous questions, but in fact did want to ask. His neighbour in a yellow sweatshirt wanted his bearded collaborator to ask, to save him doing so. The quiet in the room was comfortable. They had known each other for nearly a day, and although the course had previously hinted it could go in this direction it had taken its time getting there.

'Imagine you are all designers,' the trainer continued at last. He looked around him. The visual learners in the room needed further invitation.

'What if, for example, you were the designer of this cup.' He held a semi-transparent blue plastic water beaker up for them to see. 'How hard can it be?' he said. 'You just design a piece of plastic that curls around the sides and then stick a piece of round plastic on the bottom. A cup.

'But what if the designer of this cup is not satisfied by this. He considers that there must be something missing from the finished cup but cannot, at first, think what. Then he drills a small hole in the bottom of his cup and finally pours water in it to test the design. The water escapes from the cup and onto the leg of his trouser. Can the designer blame the cup for its inbuilt frailties?'

The man with the artistically constructed beard snorted and his friend in a yellow sweatshirt to his right joined in. One of the quieter delegates, who wore a cap pulled hard down over his eyes, raised his head for the first time in an hour and looked at the trainer, who didn't answer his own question.

'Let me give you another example,' he said instead. 'What about the designer of the jet engine. He has just spent five years sweating over original designs, amendments and prototypes. Fan blades, cooling system, cowling, everything; the lot. Finally it is ready. He looks at the lead that runs to the plug with a switch that will turn it all on for the first time. It has been years in the making, a seminal moment, one that may change not only his life but those of millions of others.

'Yet somehow he is not satisfied. It just doesn't look finished. His assistant has gone for coffees so they can sit down together and discuss the final moments before the switch is thrown. He ponders and ponders, and then realises: no badger.'

The man in the cap looked up again. A woman in purple leggings sniggered softly, not entirely aware what had amused her.

'He gets a badger from his bag and carefully inserts it into the engine. His assistant returns just as the designer completes his task and turns to him. "Ready to start it up?" he asks. "Sure," his assistant responds. "Go on," says the designer, "you do the honours."

'The assistant goes over to the switch and, with a small swagger of ceremony, pushes down the switch attaching to the lead that will fire up the jet engine for the first time. Nothing happens. Confused and dismayed, the assistant waggles the switch another couple of times. "I don't get it," he says, "it must work. Everything is right."

'The assistant runs over to join the designer at the front of the lifeless jet engine. Together they stare into the air intake. Then the assistant spots it. Black and grey and patient, towards the right of the fuel injection system at the back of the engine. "What is that doing there?" he exclaims. "What?" says the designer. "Badger. There's a *badger* in the engine." The designer looks at his co-worker serenely. "I know," he says, "I put it there."

'I guess my question is: can the designer blame the engine or, indeed, the badger?' The trainer surveyed his audience. 'He is the designer. He can hardly blame his designs for the consequences of his work.'

The woman in the purple leggings sniggered again, this time more freely. She was joined by most of the group. The trainer smiled along, content to wait his time. The man in the cap was also smiling, but not at the badger story. He had made contact. It was 4.50, time for the trainer to say what he had been leading up to.

'What if you are all designers? You don't design cups or jet engines; you design your own lives. Your design is the map and your lives follow along. Everything will turn out exactly as you design it.'

'Our brains can do all that?' The woman sitting beside the man in the cap asked her first question of the day. The trainer turned to look at her. He had noticed before that her eyes were the same startling colour as the brooch she wore. He could not know that his father had known her mother.

'Your brain is a complex but ultimately simple machine,' he answered her, 'and it will do precisely as it is told. If you ask it why you are so bad at something – a relationship, your life, *anything* – it will carry out what you programme it to do. It will

119

list all the reasons why you are so bad.'

'The switch,' the woman with ice blue eyes muttered. She didn't know where she had got this from, but somewhere in her imagination she could see the enquiring brown eyes of a badger.

'The switch,' repeated the trainer, apparently connecting with the meaning of these two words. 'If you ask your brain about opportunities, possibilities, how to succeed, what to do to get there, it will do that; exactly as it is programmed. It will list the ways and means, engaging your imagination en route.

'But *you* are the designer and you decide on the programming. If this is who you are and you are designing all of your lives, don't you think you have to be careful what you think, how you design?'

'Does this fit in with all of this positive thinking stuff?' asked the bearded man. His friend in the yellow sweatshirt was relieved. He had wanted to ask that.

'If you want it to,' answered the trainer. 'You are the designer; anything can fit into whatever you like.'

'I think I'd like to design myself a nice white yacht.' He smiled through his beard and some of the group joined him. No one noticed but the man in the cap glanced out of the window and from somewhere conjured a memory of another man who had told him about a dream of a yacht.

'Tell me,' said the trainer, 'does anyone in the world have a yacht like the one you would design?'

'Sure.'

'Well, how do you think they got it?'

'By being luckier and better than me, I guess.' As soon as he said this he knew how the man in the chair looking straight back at him would respond. The girl with the pigtails and his friend with the sweatshirt knew too. A man on the end of the circle, with the inquisitive wing of a tattooed eagle peeping out from under the left sleeve of his T-shirt, also knew. The trainer left them all to know the answer for themselves.

'You know what, I reckon the lucky bastard with this yacht doubted he could have one, right up until the moment he realised that he was going to get it.' Everyone turned to the man in the cap who had said this, virtually his first intervention of the day. It was a toss-up between him and the near silent woman with the brooch for the quietest contribution on the course so far.

'Yes, the design changed the moment he changed the way he thought.' The woman adding this to the conversation crossed her purple leggings as she spoke. The man in the yellow sweatshirt realised this was an entirely inappropriate time to look again at her breasts, but they had been interesting him all day. He had no idea why a compellingly vivid video of German girls playing beach volleyball started playing in his head at that moment.

'Shit! You have to be really careful how you think about stuff,' his friend said. His yellow-clad neighbour started at this, wondering how his thoughts could be read so easily. The girl in the purple leggings unconsciously crossed her arms.

Once again silence lapped around the room. The group appeared lost in thought and for at least two of them there was a realisation that the thoughts they were lost in were the beginnings of a blueprint that would define the next part of their lives. A moment or two of comfortable quiet followed.

'I've been thinking about your homework,' the trainer said at last.

'Homework? What are we, eleven?' The owner of the curious eagle in the seat closest to the right hand of the trainer had been quiet for the last half-hour. He had really enjoyed the morning session, but the afternoon had closed in on him like a hungry pride of lions. He was already designing himself his first cold lager of the evening.

'I was thinking maybe two or three questions to muse over in the bar,' the trainer said pleasantly.

The questions the tattooed man on the end of the group was thinking of were all framed around the phrase, 'Can you put that on my room bill?' He didn't want to think any more. In spite of some new inner voices his atavism was calling him home. His designer didn't do the evening shift.

Opposite him, on the other end of the open circle, a man who had once written an unread poem about an eagle while sitting in a small crumbling hut on a hillside watched the group of strangers around him. He had received the invitation to 'Design Your Future Life' late, but decided this was the way he wanted to continue the process of rebuilding his own. The feelings of anticipation had continued to build during the day, and he felt as if he was awaiting the emergence of a parade from round a corner. He liked these people, enjoyed the dynamic developing among them. Following his heart stutter that morning, he'd had a tingly feeling in his arms and the nape of his neck which had come and gone during the course of the day. He knew his emerging self well enough to recognise this as a sign that something important was about to happen. It was an instinct he would learn to trust, but not for another four or five years. Right now he looked around the room for clues.

The bearded man and his friend in the sweatshirt had dropped the defensive wall they had formed in front of the trainer for the first two hours of the day. Their approach to the content of the course, at first visceral and aggressive, had turned benign before becoming accepting and even eager. They were like puppies in a cardboard box and he had watched the trainer feed them titbits and ruffle their ears as he engaged them, enticing them into the centre of the group where he used their enthusiasm to feed the debates and discussions of the day. The poet wondered if his tingly arms denoted that one of them was going to experience a personal breakthrough during these two days.

One seat away from them, the man in the cap seemed disconnected, not only from the rest of the group, but often from himself. In fact they had once sat just a few metres away from each other having separate conversations in a bar they rarely frequented.

The reluctant poet felt that the man in a cap was waiting for something, but wondered if he had even heard an announcement regretting its late arrival. He had caught the tail end of a conversation between this man and the girl with streaky fair pigtails, wherein he described his life as 'being in the clouds just beyond the rings of light where his ideas played'. The pigtailed girl nodded complicity at this imagery, but the poet caught her looking in distraction at the last chocolate muffin on the plate beside the untouched fruit bowl.

The girl in the amazing leggings, who had clearly aroused the interest of not only the yellow sweatshirted man but his tattooed rival, was a woman with a personal agenda. She had been very candid with the group from the outset, saying that she intended using the day to create an exit strategy from the company that was paying her attendance fee. She furiously noted everything during the day and twice the poet had caught sight of her workbook.

She had turned everything they had talked about into a series of interlinking images which were then made into a picture. He caught a brief glimpse of caricatures of his fellow delegates and wondered what his own thumbnail sketch looked like. The poet was fairly certain that she was the cause of his tingling neck. She sent out signals as would an automatic beacon: help me, save me, tell me, warn me, cure me. Her leg attire was an effective distraction. At times her face told a different story.

The man sitting directly opposite him, on the other side of the trainer's chair, had been the spirit of the group in the morning. He'd been their leader, exchanging banter with the trainer while winking at the group to assure them that he was actually on their side, and that they could trust him to negotiate favourable break and lunch times on their behalf. His gleaming shoes, close cropped hair and partially revealed tattooed eagle's wing hinted at a military background.

The keen willingness to take part during the morning sessions demonstrated that he was ready to return to civvy street and take his place with the latest thinking on personal development to augment his pension. The poet had watched the lines on his face flex as he mimicked the remarks and emotions of the other members of this group of strangers, unconsciously lip syncing their words as he furiously wrote out phrases and lines that he would later learn to repeat at interviews and in conversations. 'In the forces?' they would say, 'Surely not. Twenty years in the Marines? It can't be. You seem far too in tune with the outside world.' Perhaps it was this man's day, the poet thought.

The girl who wore her blonde hair tied back in pigtails appeared to be the trainer's accomplice, his lovely assistant. There was no confusion of terms for her, no fuzzy phrases to be defined. When he recommended a book she nodded, as if having recently read a review of it. She was undaunted by training acronyms and knew precisely where to put the hyphen in neuro-linguistic programming.

Her statements were a public declaration of knowledge and understanding, and when a question was asked by one of the others in the group she occasionally looked at the trainer as if to say, 'Do you want to get this one? Me or you? *You*? OK.'

The poet liked her. She was fresh and easy, a bundle of enthusiasm. She had the habit of letting out a little squeal sometimes as she laughed, and the pigtails made her look like her younger sister before entering her gothic phase. They bounced around her pink cheeks and caught the sides of the red framed glasses she wore, to scour the course manual for things she could point out that would improve the next occasion it was trained out. He was sure that she was not the cause of his tingling neck.

The poet finally let his eyes rest briefly on the woman two people to his right. She appeared reluctant to be there, diffident and timorous. Did he know her from somewhere? She and he surely couldn't inhabit the same social circles, but there was something familiar about her. She had dressed formally for an off-site course. Lawyer, he guessed, possibly a banker. She had revealed little of herself during their breaks or over lunch, and hid behind laconic pronouncements about sandwiches, the room temperature, her journey to the course; the sterile boundaries of courtesy. When the trainer had first introduced himself, revealing that he loathed the traditional ice-breaker and would not pose them the question, 'You are stuck in a lift with Elvis, which dessert would you choose?' he saw that she wrote down the word 'blancmange' on her pad. During the entire day this word was the only one that appeared on the paper in front of her. In fact she had spent the hours looking just slightly to the right of the trainer and out at the car park, as if constantly updating her plan of escape.

'Just four questions, then,' the trainer said.

The pigtailed girl nodded in affirmation that, for her, four was the perfect number and exactly what she would have chosen. One of her pigtails slapped against the left arm of the red glasses.

The woman with the brooch drew a line under the word *blancmange* and readied herself with a pencil. The tattooed man yawned deeply, stretching his arms above his head, the action pulling his T-shirt up over his stomach as well as showing the world the wing, neck and beak of the eagle.

'What three things must you do with your lives before you leave this planet?' The bearded man looked at him in enquiry.

'These three things have to be non-negotiable,' the trainer continued, 'they are not wishes or hopes; they are things you will sacrifice other important things to achieve.'

'Wow!' the beard's accomplice in the yellow sweatshirt exclaimed. 'Not too tricky, then?'

The trainer smiled; he continued.

'Question number two: what is the main reason you are on this planet?'

Even the girl in the pigtails looked up at this one. The purple-legginged girl drew a planet with the word 'reason' circling it. An image of a lager bottle flashed into the head of the man with the eagle. The poet got a flash of a marching town surrounded by swards of turf cut apart by a road carrying a tiny red car. This image disappeared as quickly as it had arrived, interrupted by a question from one of his fellow delegates.

'Can number three be about my holiday?' the bearded man asked. 'I'd like to get some sleep tonight.'

'Question three,' the trainer said. 'If your life as you are living it is a perfect reflection of your beliefs, what is it that you most believe in?'

The air conditioning spluttered again and blew a waft of icy air over the group. The woman with the blue brooch shuddered. Somewhere else, another woman safely locked away in her fortress of a house pulled a cardigan closer over her shoulders. She checked the window closest to the chair she had chosen in front of afternoon television. It was bolted shut, as it always had been. Simultaneously a commuter just getting up from his regular seat on his regular train shivered before alighting to walk home. The trainer allowed a few seconds and then continued.

'Finally, what is your dream. And this one really *can* be a dream.'

The man in the cap pulled its brim down harder over his eyes. He looked at the trainer and around at the group. It was going to be a long night.

'I don't think you can possibly say,' said the poet, 'you probably only know that the minute before you die.'

Above him, from a speaker that had no respect for bass

control, a man in large crêpe shoes solicited people to go for a little walk under the moon of love. A man at a table was mouthing the wrong words of the song over the left ear of a woman sitting opposite him. He hadn't ever sung to her before. They had only slept together last night because the man from the office she really fancied had excused himself from an evening with their crowd, complaining of indigestion.

Most of the poet's group were standing at the bar. The purple leggings had turned orange in celebration of the evening and the pigtails were now let down in waves of streaked blonde hair over shoulders. In place of the red frames, the girl squinted uncomfortably behind contact lenses and she could not quite make out the eagle's friend that had appeared on the opposite shoulder of its owner. At first glance it appeared to be a sinister behemoth, but on closer inspection she thought it may have been the word 'Chelsea' impaled on a sword.

'Question two is virtually impossible. Do you think there is only one reason?' The bearded man beside him was waiting to be served at the bar, his lucidity moistened by lager. He had struggled with the concepts alone in his room, but could think more clearly with his co-conspirators in the clique they had formed in this large impersonal room.

'But he didn't say that, did he?' The man in the cap was sitting on a stool at the bar. Since dinner he had sat there with the peak of his baseball cap pulled low over his forehead, wondering how to make the kind of conversation that appeared to come easily to most of the others in his group, as well as in other groups forming around tables in this cavernous bar. To be truthful, he felt a little isolated and apart from those around him.

They turned to him.

'How do you mean?' The question came from the girl in the orange leggings. She liked this man. She liked the fact that he did not rush to the centre of the conversation, transmitting anecdotes and opinions like some of the other men in the group, vying for the 'man most likely to' award of the evening. She also wished she could be as comfortably alone with her drink as the man in the cap clearly was.

'He asked us to think about the *main* reason we are on this planet, not the only one.'

'Same thing,' said the man, who looked as if he had shaved around the outline of his beard before dinner.

'Not really,' answered the man in the cap. He turned a beer mat over slowly in his hand as he spoke. He picked up a plate that had been lying on the bar. 'What about this? Has this got only one reason to be on the planet?'

'It's a plate,' announced the bearded man, more blatantly content than he should have been with his powers of observation.

'Or a frisbee,' said his yellow sweatshirted friend.

'Paperweight.'

'Weapon.' The man with the tattoos joined the debate. The formerly pigtailed woman looked at him darkly. She had watched him change over the course of their evening together. He had drunk so much lager, and as each glassful effortlessly disappeared he had grown snippy and aggressive.

'Decoration,' added the poet. Tattooed man shot him a look. 'Well, a number of people mount plates on the wall and regard them as art,' added the poet, defensively.

'My mother collects thimbles,' one of the girls ventured.

'It's a fucking plate,' said the bearded man.

'Or a fucking frisbee,' said his friend.

'Or it could owe its entire existence to being the subject of a conversation that helps people understand something better,' said the man in the cap.

'Would it conduct electricity?' asked the girl with orange leggings. The eagle's wing appeared again as its owner downed the remnants of his latest beer.

'The point is,' said the man in the cap, 'that its principal reason for being on the planet may not be as obvious as we thought, and it's only a plate.'

'See!' said the bearded man. But no one else in the group seemed to feel this was an argument clincher.

'What if you are so busy thinking you are only a plate that you get distracted from your main purpose?' The poet felt they were closing in on something.

The man with the tattoos suddenly picked up the plate and threw it on the floor. It shattered. The formerly pigtailed woman gasped. The poet reached out and touched her arm, and two of the others took a pace back from where they had been standing. Several people from the other groups in the bar glanced over at them.

'I guess we'll never know,' he snarled. His early pole position with the group had slipped during the afternoon. He had not managed to regain his supremacy over dinner and the drink had not helped. It had never helped him before, but each time he thought it might.

No one in their group said anything for a while. The girl in orange leggings picked up the pieces of plate from the floor and placed them on the bar. The man in the yellow sweatshirt watched her breasts as she did this. The poet wondered who might be the first one to speak.

'Anyone need a drink?' asked the tattooed man. No one answered. He ordered himself one and stepped away from the group to play on a fruit machine that had been happily singing to itself in the corner all evening.

'Has anyone come up with anything for that question?' asked the girl whose hair now hung down in waves over her shoulders.

'It was the hardest one of the four, I thought.' The bearded man had decided to concede his previously intractable position.

'He can't mean something as obvious as giving birth, or inventing the hovercraft, or writing a symphony, can he?' asked the girl in the orange leggings. 'What can he want us to say?'

The poet stepped in. 'What if he doesn't want us to say anything? What if he just wants us to *think* different things? What if we are all hurtling down the same cul-de-sac, believing that we are on the planet to conceive more people who will not be sure why they are on the planet, and who in turn make more people who find the question so tough that they focus on inventing things that enable us to take this uncertainty of purpose onto other planets?' He had been thinking this for a while. He had looked at places so beautiful, so perfect and wondered if they were only there to be looked at or lived in.

The woman with the blue brooch quietly attached herself onto the outer perimeter of their group who stood at the end of the bar. She arrived just in time to hear him say this. Her room had become too dark, too oppressive for her. She had sat and stared for two hours since dinner at the questions the trainer had asked them to consider. Each time she looked at them it raised the question that she most needed to know the answer to. The one that had, probably, drawn her to the course in the first place. Maybe it was not, after all, Human Resources who had sent her here...

She had heard this poet say a number of things during the course of the day. There was something about the way he spoke, the way he reasoned. She had no idea why she desperately wanted to ask him a question, placing a distant sense of recognition on the notion that she now wanted to get to know him.

As she picked at the label of her cold beer she looked down the line of the bar to the rest of the group. Again she had the feeling that she knew the man in the cap who was sitting on his own at the end. She recognised that the cap he was wearing granted him the level of anonymity he craved. She could scarcely have picked him out of an ID parade, even given their day of training together in the same room, but two or three times they had exchanged a look that said, 'Do I know you?' Now, at the bar, the feeling was stronger than ever.

The bottle in her hand was wet and cold, having just been taken out of the fridge. It was later in the evening than she would usually drink, and part of her wished she had never ordered it. As she listened to the conversation going on around her the label from the bottle started to slide against the wet glue that didn't quite attach it. It was an unbelievably satisfying feeling. She had just needed to pick at one corner where the glue had maintained a notional last stand and the whole thing became free to ease off the bottle. She had gently coaxed it off and now had it in her hand. She could feel the moist slippery glue on its underside and gingerly flattened it before placing it on the bar in front of her.

At that moment the poet turned to where she stood. Later she would recreate this instant in slow motion, watching his eyes take in the label lying face up on the bar with one slightly creased corner. She did not take her eyes off him as he raised his head to look at her. And then she said it.

'Do you mind if I ask you a question?'

He said he didn't mind. She knew that none of the group

could possibly hear what she asked him. She didn't see, however, that the man in the cap was watching the scene from his vantage point at the end of the bar. She asked the question.

The poet answered the question as he had answered many before. He felt good tonight. A number of people had sought his viewpoint and he had sensed the leadership of the group shift from the tattooed man to him. He did not even have time to remember or evaluate his answer as, just as he gave it, the girl with the orange leggings jogged his arm and asked him to settle an argument between her and her blatant admirer in the yellow sweatshirt. He turned back to her and, for him, instantly the moment was gone.

The man in the cap witnessed all of this. He had not heard the interchange between the poet and the woman with the ice blue brooch, but had watched her expression as they spoke. He saw the poet turn away from her, and saw her freeze. He saw her look blankly at the back of the poet, now engaged elsewhere. Saw her look away. Saw her change of countenance. He looked at the clock above the bar. It was 11.20.

He watched as the woman picked up her bottle three times and put it down again without taking a sip. Saw her pick up the label from the counter and try to stick it back on the bottle. It had lost a lot of its tackiness and refused to re-adhere. She did not exchange another word with any of her fellow delegates and eventually left the bar.

The man in the cap then watched the poet, who had two bottles of beer lined up on the bar in front of him. The group that surrounded him had forgotten the questions asked of them by the trainer, which had returned to their 'too hard' baskets, to be retrieved after breakfast the following morning. They had been so busy trying to understand what the clues were that they had forgotten to look for them. As the man in the cap got up to leave the bar he looked at a piece of paper that was lying in front of the poet. For him question two remained unanswered.

Meanwhile, the woman with the ice blue brooch paced her room. She thought and thought about what the poet had said. She wrote down her question and attached the answer he had given to it. She examined and re-examined the two together. It was as if the words took on a life of their own, rushing up at her, taking her breath away. For the second time in two days she felt dizzy and short-winded, but this time she knew why.

After two hours of turning the poet's answer over and over in her mind, she went to bed and tried to sleep. At about the same time the poet crashed into his room, wrestled feebly with his underwear, gave up on the fight and tumbled into bed. Within a minute he was asleep.

Three hours later the woman with a blue brooch lying on her bedside table got up again, having not slept a wink. She made a cup of bad tea from the ridiculous kettle on a faux wooden tray in her shabby conference-centre room. She couldn't drink it. She couldn't know that the snores she heard through the paper-thin walls of her room were those of the man who had caused her unrest. Next door the poet dreamed of avenues of trees and lines of houses, and people with no faces walking between them looking for a way out.

At five thirty, as the sun rose, she put on her clothes and walked through the grounds of the centre. There was a sharp crispness to the air of this new April morning. Two chaffinches flew in darting formation, their pink under-feathers glowing red against the early morning sky. Long wet grass licked against her bare ankles as she skirted the conference centre equivalent of a ha-ha and made her way to a hedge she had seen from the training room window the day before.

As she followed the path of the hedge she took out the piece of paper with her question and the answer written on it. She knew exactly what shape the creases in the paper had made of the words, and could see in her mind's eye the question mark that she had emboldened by drawing over it five, six, seven times.

The words of the poet resonated in her head and, finally, she knew exactly what she had to do. She ran back to her room and arrived panting at the door. In her excitement she fumbled with her keycard, inserting it in the slot five or six times before a little green light allowed her access.

She threw everything into her case, ran to her tiny red car and drove out across country roads back to the city. There was precision in her movements. Her life would never be the same.

She got back and almost instantly rang the number of the woman that had remained ignored on a pad beside her telephone for the last two months. The words 'cognitive therapy', beside the number she called, had been circled twice. She would have no more regrets, except maybe for the fact that she would love to have thanked the poet for what he said.

She never said these words to him.

The trainer glanced again at the empty chair. He noticed the change in atmosphere since last evening but had learnt not to question such things. The eagle had nested under a long-sleeved rugby shirt that bore the legend 'No Quitter', but it was in stark contrast to the body language of its wearer, who was slumped back in his chair, feet up on another placed in front of it. The purple leggings had moved chairs and now occupied the place beside the man whose yellow sweatshirt had been replaced by a blue one. The trainer noticed that she had flushed at least twice in response to shared somethings with her new neighbour, the second time giggling as he wrote a few words on a page of her workbook.

His bearded friend was animated this morning. The previous evening had exhausted but rejuvenated him. He too had made new allies, and the pigtailed girl and the poet shared answers with him as they undertook the first exercise of the morning. Where they had smiled separately yesterday at quips designed to test the boundaries between them, they now laughed together as a group of people bonded by experience.

The man in the cap also sat low in his chair. He had neither signed treaties of friendship nor declared war on his fellow delegates. He sensed the loss of the tattooed man across the room, feeling he had been defeated by more than the effects of alcohol as it strove to leave his system. The two of them had sat on separate tables over breakfast, looking down at triangles of cold white toast standing erect in their racks, not even nodding in recognition of a day shared, with one to come.

'What about question two: what is the main reason you are on the planet?' asked the trainer. 'Did anyone find an answer to this?'

'How can we ever know?' It was the poet who answered on behalf of his newly acquired team.

'Which part of you?' the trainer asked. The group puzzled over this for a while.

'Which part of us what?' responded the bearded man at last.

'Which part of you knows or does not know? Which part are you listening to when searching for an answer to question two? The part of you that is at the mercy of destiny, or the part of you that is defining it?'

'For me I think it is something I am yet to do, and yet to know,' said the poet. The tingling in his arms and neck had stopped this morning, and he put it down to the erratic air conditioning in the room the day before.

The man in the cap looked out into the car park at the space where a tiny red car had been parked the day before. Maybe you can never know, he thought.

The Child

As he jumped the last step leading to the platform there was just time for the master commuter to take in the information required to make his decision. The 'Arrivals' indicator winked at him conspiratorially. 'Train Approaching', it flashed, and with the practised eye of a man familiar to the territory of rail travel, his look swept to the front of the train announcing its arrival at the station with a griping squeal of brakes. The luck that, just twenty minutes ago, had permitted a globe of leaping orange juice to get jogged out of his glass, described a parabola in the air and conspired with gravity to miss the white sleeve of his shirt, and just eleven harried minutes later to take the flattened face of Elizabeth Fry at first attempt into the ticket machine, held firm. The approaching train was his. There would be no need for him to get a later train and so squeeze onto the crowded platform five stops later and change trains at a time when seats were currency. On the later service his position by the door could be challenged by those wealthy enough to afford tiny flats and Monopoly-sized houses closer to the centre. Odd to think he could now buy them all with loose change.

He sat on the seat he had made his own on many journeys in the past five years. He no longer needed to work, everything had changed, but he needed the certainty of the commute, of this part of his life he could still control.

The signs that predicted this was going to be a good day got even better. There was a discarded newspaper folded and wedged into the gap where the upholstery ended and the chipped Formica side of the body of the carriage began. He took it out and turned to the sports section at the back, unconsciously checking the page whose corner had been neatly turned down to remind the previous reader of an important something she would have remembered had she not forgotten to take the paper with her as her station appeared before she expected.

Sitting opposite him was a man whose face he may have recalled, had its features not appeared in assorted varieties on every eighth person he had ever met. In fact this was the stranger who had forcibly held the electric doors of the train open for him eleven months previously, causing its hydraulic signature to puff and pant, relenting to the shoulder being pressed against it and finally spring back open to enable him to escape the carriage.

'Stand clear, *stand clear!*' a guard had hollered after him, trying as best he could to look officious in a turquoise uniform with elaborate shoulder braiding.

'Thanks,' he had muttered over his shoulder in the general direction of the stranger as he scrambled off, the papers he had hurriedly gathered up from his lap gripped in the fist he had made in the stress of the moment.

Had this man not held the door for him he would have been forced to disembark one station on, change platforms, wait for a return train and walk home twenty minutes later. He would then have been pulped against the safety barriers of the road just down from his home by a lorry bursting a tyre against a curb, careering off its path, destroying the central reservation and slamming harmlessly against the railings on the other side of the street. As it is he had, two days later, unwittingly skim-read a four-line article about this lame and forgettable incident in an edition of the paper he was now reading.

This morning, sitting two seats away from the man who had saved his life, was a woman the master commuter recognised not only as a fellow traveller, but as someone he had known as the wife of a friend. He found her fearsome and unforgiving, but he would never have wished on her the horror her life had become. He knew why she wore the hood of her fleece like a cowl. Beneath it, hollow eyes now red but once nearly as blue as the brooch she wore on the jacket it covered, backed into her face above grey bags that barely contained the tears of the last endless years.

He knew she didn't recognise him, lost in her grief, despite the fact they sat within recognising distance. He wondered if he had ever seen any other expression on her face than despair. A woman who didn't realise that the key she needed to forgive herself and learn to move on was permission only she could grant. She would begin to discover this tomorrow from a near stranger when it was perfect for her to know it, but for now sat with her head down, shunning her fellow passengers, dreading the day just started, and despising the thought of the training course she was being forced to attend the next day.

On the lap of another woman a couple of seats away from her was a baby living behind an old man's face, worry lines pre-programmed into his ancestral DNA. It was a baby who had not yet learnt that he could not have dessert before his main course, or that wet Saturday mornings were a thing to be reviled. His life was still fresh with hope and free from the limitations of those who would programme him. He would save the life of the master commuter in thirty-eight years' time, performing pioneering arterial microsurgery on a man he would know to be a complete stranger; another millionaire client to sate his passion for Comex Submariners and Chateau Haut-Brion.

Oblivious to all of this, but transfixed by a newspaper report of a score in a game he had no interest in, the master commuter glanced away from his paper and looked blankly around the carriage. It had been a strange morning. Who was the man on the platform of the tube he had felt compelled to look at as he ascended the stairs to the platform? Did he recognise him? He had looked hard and had to shake his head to disentangle himself from the momentary connection they had made. His shock of ginger hair and legendary grumpiness had attracted multiple levels of negative attention as a kid, but it had been a while since someone had stared at the now lightly gelled adult version.

There was something different about the day. He noticed that the train carriage seemed very empty for a Monday. His eyes trailed around, landing on a poster that proclaimed to be 'Poems on the Overground'. It bore its message prosaically. 'Breathe through your eyes,' it said and was signed simply 'Simon'. Hardly Keats, he thought, but nevertheless closed his mouth, making his eyes sting with the effort of trying to suck air in through them. He inhaled quickly, glancing around at his fellow passengers to spot if any of them had caught him in his rather too literal application of Simon's wisdom.

He failed to spot a fellow passenger four seats to his right blink rapidly as he got up to leave the train, squinting purposefully to readjust his contact lenses as he rose, while catching the breath he, too, had held. The master commuter also failed to notice the smiling baby down the carriage; glee conjured by what the baby thought was a version of the winking game the man his mother said was his 'uncle' played with him. The baby didn't know it was a stranger he was smiling at, and could not know that he would be sued by him in thirty years' time for malpractice following an surgical procedure that left this man, his patient, lame, and which would stop him boarding a plane that would crash, killing all on board.

The master commuter evaluated the day that lay ahead of him. It was one that was typical of the life he led before the win. One that kept him away from his stuttering marriage. Glancing at his watch he realised that, with a following wind, he should just make the first of three meetings on time. There was not a lot of meat on the skeleton of his timetable, but if he sacrificed the niceties of synchronised road walking and put faith in his deodorant he could arrive looking cool and perfectly timed in the reception of the first client. He had the notes with him somewhere. He mentally searched his briefcase and found them inside a blue folder, wedged in between his laptop and the file that would arm him with information for his second meeting of the day. He remembered packing the file last night and knew that he would have to review the notes of their get-together a month earlier, before tipping up informed with the data this client required.

Organising the day in the front of his mind, he momentarily glanced out of the window and saw two women on a platform hunched over too much luggage. He caught them pulling tighter over their slight gym-toned frames the skimpy outfits they had chosen when scouting websites for forecasts of their much longed-for holiday destination. They had studiously ignored the fact they would spend a whole day of an English April getting to the airport and being delayed by thirty hours in an overactively air-conditioned terminal building, clutching tokens for 'tea and one savoury item' from a 24-hour canteen that closed at ten. The woman in pink, who could have been the mother, sister, friend or rival in love of the one in blue, held her fourth cigarette of the day down close against her thigh as she huddled against a cold concrete pillar for warmth. She would not discover the burn mark in her three-quarter pastel pink trousers until three days into their holiday. She would blame her companion, and they would fight over that and a gaggle of other issues that had gathered steam over the years. One of these issues was the man who was half observing them with unseeing eyes; a man the woman in pink had spotted in a bar eight years ago and pointed him out to her companion in blue. As the woman in pink had gone to the ladies to finalise her approach strategy, her blue rival had made a move that was repelled only two days later by a master commuter who had made worse mistakes in love.

Unaware of this, as to the history of another, the man on the train looked back at the briefcase on the seat beside him. He had not noticed, but the woman and baby had got off the train at the last stop. His friend's ex-wife, brooch pinned tightly to her lapel, alighted by a different exit at the same time. She needed to breathe. She ached with the effort of living her life. She decided there and then to go back to commuting by car and braving the M4, with its endless stream of winking lights and solitary drivers who sat hypnotised by the road ahead that they followed for ever. He was wrong, she had recognised the ginger commuter, but now wasn't the time. She was sure that the time would be never. She was wrong. They had designed it differently.

Back on the train, the master commuter mentally ticked off the phone calls that had to be made in either the interval, if such a thing arrived, between his first and second meetings, or before the final meeting at three thirty, the most challenging item on the day's agenda. He knew that he would have to be on top form for that one. The woman on the other side had been a monster before, virtually notching the points she scored on the leg of a wild but sleek zebrano desk. He recalled that in their meeting room, her office, the blinds behind her were pulled tightly closed against a huge ornate Victorian bay window, only accentuating the effect of two halogen lights set on sentry poles behind her head and aimed at his chair.

The impact of this heavily rehearsed place of interrogation and execution was bizarre. When entering the grand but narrow room the first sighting of her had been like that of a funnel-web spider hunched silently at the end of the tapering vault that acted as her web. The lights behind her head picked out a halo of fine brown hairs that had escaped the throng around her cheeks, while the sphere occupied by her face was in total shadow. At first it was impossible to work out if she was facing towards or away from him, and throughout their meeting he found he could not respond to expressions he couldn't see.

She had sat tapping at the keyboard of her computer for two or three minutes following his entry into her domain. There had been no chair in front of the desk to sit on and he spent this time looking down at her hands as they worked, bathed blue by the light of the screen.

As he stood there seeking an entry visa she said, without raising her head, 'There's a chair against the wall. You can sit on it.' He flipped his head left and right searching for the furniture she referred to, finding it in a ring of light where the two halogen beams met. It was a low Gothic piece, lumpily upholstered in coarse red cloth, with a high back ostentatiously carved in dark mahogany waves. It was either too heavy to move or fixed to the floor where it rested, he could not decide. After two half-hearted attempts to move it closer to the desk where the spider waited, neither of which she acknowledged, he accepted his time in the spotlight. This is where he stayed for the twenty minutes of their meeting, unlearning all of the tips and techniques that had brought him sales awards over the last ten years.

He had known the meeting was over when she resumed her tapping.

'We'll meet again,' she said without looking up, 'Arcadia will email you.'

He had murmured something fatuous like, 'OK', or 'That's good then', towards the shadowed face and blue hands before shuffling back towards the door. Somewhere deep inside him someone wondered what would happen if, before leaving, he reached across and dropped the heavy carved glass paperweight to the left of her hands into the coffee cup to the right, or if he leaned in and just gently tweaked her nipple, making a honking noise as he did so. What would she do? What kind of reaction would there be? He felt himself shudder at the thought as he emerged from the funnel.

Arcadia had emailed him. There had been a brief negotiation about possible meeting arrangements, in that he had suggested four times and dates convenient to him and agreed to one that wasn't. He had moved three things he should have done instead and this afternoon at three thirty he would return to the monster's lair.

Despite the feelings the meeting had aroused in him at the time, he wanted to go back. It was what he did and today he felt good.

After the win and his eventual escape from the island he had not felt good for the longest time. He could not locate 'good' in any part of his new life, so reverted quickly back to familiar territory.

As the train clanked and rattled on, he lined up the targets of his day. He knew he should have checked in his briefcase for the blue file, and made a note of the phone calls, making (what had they called them?) 's.m.a.r.t. objectives' for each one, but somehow he couldn't. The agenda of his day spread before him like a journey back from the sea at the time of the tide turning. There would be channels to hop, and deepening pools to circumnavigate, but he would find a route to get to where he needed to be. It was almost sport to him. It had kept him going since she had left him, alone with this sport and his empty millions. He looked up again and saw two more people leave the train.

'I don't want to go.' When the child spoke it was as if the words came from nowhere. The master commuter had been so engrossed in his plans for the day that he had forgotten to give any thought to the needs of the child. His stomach felt suddenly hollow, as if plummeting to the ground in an overenthusiastic lift. He could almost see the stress lines in their relationship stretching out in front and all around them, marking out boundaries he thought they had settled before.

'What do you mean?' It was all he could think of to say.

The child emitted a shudder. This was words. Sometimes

there weren't words, only feelings. His feelings were that he did not want to go.

The man felt the child's resistance. As the train piled on he looked for a landmark to get a sense for where they were on their journey. Stations had fled past during the ticking of his internal checklist and now he felt oddly disoriented. He saw the basin full of barges and boats. This was usually an uplifting segue on his journey in. It always seemed to appear as if out of nowhere: two dilapidated warehouses, their windows shattered, brickwork muddied by the sooty streaks of millions of passing cars gave way to a vehicle breaker's yard and finally, round a corner, the basin emerged. It was surrounded by apartment blocks apparently designed by children to sport pink bricks with bright blue balcony rails hanging over the water as if to constantly check it was still there, this oasis in an industrial suburb.

It had been marketed as 'a redevelopment initiative', but to the herons who dived there, surprised to discover their lunch had reappeared in this most unexpected place, it was like an emerald dot on a grey page seen from above.

Today the water seemed unfathomable and the barges it lapped against dingy and forlorn. The doors of the apartments were slammed closed on the basin as the wind whistled through tatty patio furniture that huddled in leaf-strewn corners fending off swirling litter and pigeons sheltering from the rain. Before the win, escaping his vacuous marriage, he had often played out a fantasy of living there, having his breakfast on his balcony on a Saturday morning as his neighbour in a holiday robe passed a fresh brioche through the jolly blue railing separating their apartments.

'Try this,' she would say, 'I bought it at the baker's down the street. It's yummy.'

The child shrugged. He knew he had to try again.

'You do want to go. It will be fun.' He knew this wasn't a persuasive line to take, but hoped that it would at least buy him a little time.

The child shrank into the shadows. The train was making a shrieking noise that he didn't like. It was shaking about too much. He wondered what it would take for it to fall off the rails. He remembered looking inside one of his trains, the yellow one, at home when it had fallen off the rails to see what had happened to the people in there. There had been no seats, though, nowhere for people to sit. His tummy felt funny, like there was nothing in it, and it kept making an aching sound. His head felt funny too. He didn't want to go.

'What's wrong with you all of a sudden? You haven't made a fuss like this for ages.' The man tried to hide his exasperation, but it was tough. This was not the time. It was less than ten minutes before the train was due to arrive, and all of his deadlines were already running on fumes. He didn't need to fight a reluctant child, dragging it around like emotional ballast as he took on the tube.

'I don't like it,' the child said, his voice small with worry.

'What? What exactly don't you like? What *is* it?'

'You know,' said the child. He must know, he thought, he was an adult. He didn't know himself, and these questions didn't help. He felt bad. Horrible. There was that noise again. All of this frightened him, he…

'What is it? What are you afraid of?' the man asked. He hadn't wanted to put the question, not wanting to introduce words like 'afraid' into the conversation. There just wasn't the time, and this was hardly the place.

The child shrugged again. His breath was now shorter. He could hear it in his throat. His hands were going tingly. His head felt big.

'*What?*' The man knew he was using a bullying technique to elicit a response. Why? Bugger it, because he could. Why else do bullies bully? He also knew that this tactic might scare the answer into a corner too far away to be found. It might buy him the time he needed to get on with his day and hit his targets. There would be time later for this.

'Everything,' the child said suddenly.

'*What?* Everything what?' The question didn't make any sense, but neither had the child's response. Small ginger hairs stood up, at red alert, on his arms.

'But that is nonsense,' he told the child, 'this is a great day, exciting even. These aren't scary people, they are just people.

Come on, there have been loads worse than this. That presentation last week, for instance, that was terrible. Today? It's just a walk in the park. What's the worst that can happen?'

The child trembled as snapshots of the bad things that had happened filled the frames of the comic book in his head. He had lain in bed thinking about those times, counting back in sevens from 400 to shake them away. Then the dark had come. It started in the corners of his room and spread out towards him as the light went away. The worst that could happen was this feeling, being frightened and not knowing when it would stop. *This* was the worst.

'It's you!' he cried.

'What is?'

'This is. Everything. It's *you*. Making me do this when I don't want to.'

'You have to.' But as soon as he said it he knew he had made a mistake.

The child felt as if he had lost control of his head. Everything seemed suddenly far away and fuzzy, although he could still see the edges of everything as sharp as before. The tingle had spread to the tops of his arms. His fingers felt heavy and empty, as if someone else was controlling them. He started to breathe in short pants and the breath stopped in his throat which was dry and narrow.

'No,' he said, 'no, *no!*' He looked desperately around the carriage. He wondered what the black bits on the inside edges of the doors would feel like if he pulled at them. He needed to get out. To get away. He had to *go*.

'Look, tell me about it. What is it you don't like?'

'You know.' They had returned to this place.

He made himself think about what the therapist had told him in that pale, unruffled room.

'Speak to the child,' she had said. He had looked at her.

'How, how do I speak to him? What do I say?'

'It is not what you want to say, but what the child hears that is important. What do you think the child wants to hear?'

He had searched inside himself. How could he know? It had been so long since he had been a child. What was the language of

143

children? How was it different to that of the adults most of them became? What did this child need him to say? Whatever had happened between them that led the child to ask such questions?

'I know,' he said at last. 'I know.' And he thought he might. The panting felt as if it had slowed a little.

'You can trust me, you know.'

'I can't,' said a small voice.

'Why not? You know I love you.'

'So did she. She said she loved me, but she went away.'

'She didn't want to,' he said, 'she really, really loved you. Sometimes adults, even mummies, can't do what they most want. She didn't want to go away. She was ill, very ill. She never stopped thinking about you. Never stopped loving you.'

'She did,' whispered the child, 'she went away. She wouldn't have gone away if she loved me.'

'She couldn't help it. She was ill. And she came back.'

'Not for a long time,' said the child.

The man knew that they were seeing the truth from opposite corners of the room. It looked different to him.

'I am not going away,' he said. 'I love you and I am never going away. You can trust me.'

'I can't.'

It was hardly said, barely audible, but he knew this was the child's truth. It was a matter of trust. It had always been a matter of trust. He was thirty-seven and it was the greatest and latest lesson he had learnt; or at least it was one he was constantly learning. He had turned his life around, and not just with millions of pounds. Through painful experience, and despite constantly returning to his original mistrusting and suspicious state of mind he had, as an adult, learnt to trust the collective unconscious he called the universe. Then the more he trusted, the more this trust was justified; and the more he trusted.

Sometimes he would stop trusting and return to what he was starting to question as his default position. Having fled the boat and the island his trust had been shattered. It felt for a while it would never return. Later he started to trust again, saw the results, gave himself feedback on these and learnt another lesson. Trusting meant not judging the consequences.

The trust he offered had to be unconditional. Part of him was beginning to learn that he couldn't trust and then question the manner, timing and extent of the delivery. When he had questioned it in this way, wondering why things did not appear in the nature of the script he told himself he would prefer, he had a sense that the universe simply paused quietly, waiting for his trust to become unconditional. And sometimes he gave it, recognised the results and gradually redrew the lines of conflict within himself.

It was the hardest lesson. Now, with just five minutes remaining of his journey as they rattled together towards the centre, he remembered a time a year ago when a notable clue had been delivered. Sure, he had failed to trust since, but it was no longer his natural form. It was if trust had entered his body like an antivirus and was reprogramming him as he learnt.

The clues had gathered on an early spring afternoon just like this one, last year. The end of another tough day found him exhausted at some airport or other. He had been returning from somewhere and ushered into the steel and neon environment by automatic doors that slid apart to reveal the onomatopoeic centre of the world. The ping of security arches, the whoosh of air conditioning units aping the roar of their much more impressive cousins out on the tarmac oozed over the zing, gleam and shine of the myriads of surfaces that bore tickets, coupons, luggage, advertisements and everything else that made up the sleek chaos of modern air travel.

A woman with a smile so big it almost touched the wayward edge of her jauntily angled hat checked him into a window seat. She led his gaze to the tiny rucksack he produced as evidence that he had nothing to check into the hold of the aircraft. No, he had not left his luggage unattended and yes, he had packed it himself. No, it did not contain any sharp objects and yes, he had considered the almost limitless possibilities the Frequent Flyers' Fiesta Forever Scheme offered him.

'Four Fs,' she assured him, broadening her smile so it took up two of the seats in the smoking area beside check-in, 'means that you are never more than ten flights away from a free gift.'

He searched his pockets, clothing, imagination and rucksack

for some interest in this fact but failed to locate any.

'I came back from Minorca and got an ironing board,' she followed through. 'It's lovely.'

He tore himself away and lined up behind a man at the security X-ray machines who had sedulously emptied all of his pockets of coins, keys, tissues and blobs of pale blue lint, only to send the detection machines wild as he walked through. He had only wondered at this man's look of total puzzlement as he presented himself to be frisked when the search revealed a plank-sized chisel inside his jacket. He left the scene as one of the security officers was donning a pair of protective rubber gloves with rather too much zeal and enthusiasm. However, he still felt a residue of reluctance. He remembered another conversation at a similar security gate when his ex-wife had asked him whether knitting needles were regarded as dangerous objects. But this memory predated all that. His ex-wife was still his wife and the plane he was catching was not taking him to Antigua.

On this flight, his irrational fear of in-flight catering led to him stocking up on two Danish and a coffee that was more froth than promise, and he made his way towards the window that framed the bustle of activity on the apron outside. He was settling down to watch people riding airport vehicles like dodgems around painted lines on this enormous concrete arena when his phone rang. 'Wife' the screen said.

'Hello, wife,' he said picking at a piece of flaked icing sugar on his jacket sleeve.

'They want three and a half grand,' she announced. This was a tactic she had adopted fairly early on in the unspoken negotiations of their relationship; she would start a phone conversation in mid-sentence and dare him to fill in the salutation.

'Who do?' he asked.

'And they want it by the end of next week or we will lose the mortgage. And frankly I don't care if we do. The whole thing is getting out of hand. It's a preposterous sum of money to borrow and a ludicrous amount of what they call "introductory commission".' He could actually hear the inverted commas. 'This is yours. I wash my hands of it.'

'Breaking up,' he said. He had acquired annoying habits of his own.

'What?' she said. 'Where are you?'

'Hard to do,' he said.

'What?' she said again.

'Breaking up,' he repeated.

'Are you messing around with me? Didn't you hear what I said?'

'I heard,' he answered. 'The bank want their fee by next week or we'll lose the mortgage.'

The phone was an excellent instrument for magnifying the lack of sound at one or other end of it. His wife had clearly changed tack here. It worked.

'How much do they want?'

'I just told you. Three and a half grand. By the end of next week.'

'We'll sort it,' he said. 'We can do this. It's important to us.' He put calm in his voice. He didn't know how well it would transmit over the ambient sounds of a departure lounge at an airport. The gurgle of an espresso machine and the thump of packages marked 'fragile' being hurled into the belly of an Airbus outside joined the orchestra of announcements by a woman with a mouthful of spoons.

'No, we won't sort it, *you* will. This is your idea. You sort it.'

'I will,' he said.

'Listen to me,' her voice became insistent, '*you* sort it. Not the "universe" or any other higher than us bloody omni-force. *You*. Did you hear me? *You*.'

The word 'universe' had been spat out like a bone from a morsel of fish. He understood her. She had looked at him with hooded eyes as he did all he could to explain the epiphany of trust he had swathed himself in. She had seemed open to what he was saying, but he could see the tablecloth tighten under the knife, fork and side plate on the table. She was clutching at it with her hands out of sight. Trying.

There were times she would listen and nearly hear, and there were times she wouldn't listen, as if unwittingly waiting for a man in a boat. Then there were times she would shout because she knew she was doing it for nine wasted years. Then there was this time.

'I will do something about it. Trust me.'

'You,' she said. 'You. Not the universe. *You*.' She ended the call. The beep that signalled the end of the call was just another death knell in a relationship he had forgotten how to save. For all his new-found trust, he only fired blanks in the gunfight with his wife.

For a short while after she rang off, he had thought about worrying about it. He sort of thought about making a list. He nearly realised that none of this was what he did any more before he completely forgot to do either of those things. He watched two men down on the ground look at the blade of a Fokker 50. They turned it round slowly as they chatted. A ray of sun escaped the gloom and glinted off one of the propellors as he looked at the clouds and wondered for the thousandth time what it would be like to break through and fly above them. His trust went through the hole in the sky from which the ray of sun had emerged.

After they landed he had checked his watch. 5.20. He would be home by half seven. He undid his seat belt before the captain had turned the engines off and thought about opening up the tray table from the seat in front of him to see what reaction he could provoke from the cabin crew who were busy preparing their smiles for disembarkation. He then retrieved his phone from the rucksack as he stood in the aisle, jostling for position with everyone else who wanted to be first to the next delay on their journey.

He turned on the phone discreetly, even though he had been commanded not to do so before he had reached the terminal building. Within seconds it beeped at him. He had one new message. He pointedly did not check carefully for any baggage or personal belongings that he might have left on the plane and called his message service.

'Hello. This is Amanda Chambers. You know Amanda from Silo? I hope you remember, you carried out some consultancy for us about, what was it, three years ago and I am desperate for a bit of help. Do you still do that? Maybe you can call me.

'Look. I am here in the office until five thirty (it's Wednesday, by the way) and I really have to speak to you. It's urgent. Can you call me?'

She left her number at the end of the message. He checked his watch. It was 5.23. He stood on the air bridge and became one of those men he had accidentally banged his bag against who simply had to make a call as soon as they emerged from the plane, and who could not possibly wait until they reached the arrivals hall. He called her. She answered. That hardly ever happened.

'Hello, Amanda.' He announced himself and heard the relief in her voice.

'I'm desperate, I really need your help. I have been told by Bob, do you remember Bob? "Bob the Bastard" you used to call him. Anyway, Bob says that we need someone to help us out next week. Huge main board presentation in New York (could be Cape Town) the week after. What would that be? The 23rd? Could you make it? I have the budget and can sign cheques. The budget expires on Monday so you wouldn't have to wait for ages. You could have it now if you wanted. Can you do it?'

He mentally checked his diary. He could move things around next week. He liked her. He even liked Bob a bit. He liked the work she was asking him to do; sales presentations could be fun. He could do it next week, he told her.

'Fantastic!' she cried out. 'Oh, but I have a tiny problem. Well, maybe massive. Huge. I can't do your daily rate of, what was it, sixteen hundred? I have begged for this and they gave me all they could.'

'What do you have for this?' he asked her.

Her voice got smaller; he missed the number she nearly whispered as two children emerged from the aircraft and tore up the gangway, using up the energy they had saved by only kicking the seats in front of theirs gently for the entire duration of the flight. He asked her to repeat it. She misunderstood the reason for the request.

'I am really sorry,' she said, 'but you can have a cheque for it now, if you like. Or cash? Would you prefer cash?'

'No, I didn't hear how much you said.'

'3,500 for the three days. But we can pay your travel.'

He almost forgot to wonder at the apparent coincidence of this. However, it hadn't been that long, and what he had always though of as his default position was lurking somewhere in the shadows. Something in him, maybe his instinct, saw this as a clue.

He decided to pass it on to someone else.

'Could you do me a favour, Amanda?'

'Of course. Yes, absolutely. What is it?'

'Are you really able to write out a cheque tonight for this?'

'Sure.' He could hear a rustling sound and could picture her taking a chequebook out of the drawer. He felt he could hear her showing it to the phone.

'Could you write me a cheque for the 3,500 and send it out tonight?'

'You'll want the VAT with that, won't you?'

'That's just the thing,' he replied. 'Can I have the VAT by a separate cheque? You can make that one out later.'

Amanda went quiet on the phone.

'This isn't tax evasion or anything bad, Amanda. You know me. I can explain it to you all when I see you next week.'

'OK,' she said, 'anything else?'

'Actually, yes. Could you get it couriered over to me at my home address? It's the same as when I was last with you. If you could do that for me right away we have a deal.'

'Anything else?' she asked. She was back in her comfort zone now; efficient, helpful, needed. In control.

'Well, just one more tiny thing. Could you please just put a simple note in with the cheque for me?'

'A note?'

'Yes. Could you please just write, "Love from the universe" on the note. Can you do that for me, Amanda?'

He could hear her thinking.

He wasn't really ever going to explain this. He wasn't completely sure what he would say in any event. He knew she would agree and guessed that she would almost certainly never ask him to expand on it.

'Love from the universe?'

Yes, he thought.

'Thanks, Amanda.'

He looked again at his watch. 5.44. The cabin crew had disappeared back inside the body of the aircraft. He was alone on the air bridge apart from a man with a clipboard who was writing down numbers that would be entered into a grid to compete with all the other numbers for the title of useless data of the day. The man pushed a button on the inside of the plane by the door. This button existed to be pushed by men with clipboards. It complied by changing to green to his touch. '11, 20,' he wrote, dotting the last number in satisfaction with the point of his pen. He went off whistling to enter the data back in a room with no windows.

5.44, he thought. He would be home before eight. The courier would surely be there before that. He knew his wife would be home. He knew she would open the envelope. He did not know what she would think. He hoped that she would smile; he hadn't seen her do that in a while.

He made his way towards the arrivals' lounge. People were waiting there to get on the plane to reverse his journey and deliver their own surprises. He found himself whistling the same tune as the man with the clipboard as he whisked past them.

Almost an hour and a half and two tubes later he reached his front door. He let himself in and saw an envelope lying opened on the stand beside the door next to the candles and the pot for loose change. He peered inside the hall and could see his wife's head above the back of the sofa in the sitting room where she was watching television.

As he moved towards the doorway she turned her head. He saw the cheque lying on the table beside the sofa, a note lying under it almost completely obscured. She followed his gaze down to the table and looked at him in a way that made him realise things had probably become terminal between them.

'Bastard!' she said.

That was the moment he decided his new default position on trust needed to upgrade. His eye left the ball and he started to externalise. He began his fixation with buying his wife back, away from trust and towards six little numbers that spelled out his dream.

A year and a million changes later, on the train heading towards the centre, he nearly smiled at the memory of the universal cheque, but knew there was no time. Learning to trust is one thing, he thought. Trying to teach it is something very different. It could not be taught, only experienced.

'Do you know what I do when I am afraid?' he asked.

The child waited. It was not what he had expected.

'When are you afraid?'

'Many times. Sometimes I think it is all the while, but it is just that I have become accustomed to it.'

The child squinted. What was *that* word?

'*Used* to it. I think I become used to that feeling.'

'What do you do?'

'I make a list in my head of all the times I have felt good. Then I remember that I felt good sometimes after feeling scared. So being scared was not the end of things. It was just a feeling.' He waited for a reaction, but didn't get one. The butterflies were still prodigious and flying out of formation. 'What do you think the child wants to hear?' the therapist had asked him.

'It's because of that feeling I want to promise you something.'

'What is it?' the child said.

'I promise you that if you feel at all uncomfortable or scared during the day we will turn around and go somewhere else.'

You cannot teach trust, you have to experience it, find it within you. To recognise it you have to know it when you have it. The only way to know it is to feel it. The child neither knew nor felt trust. His mother had been sick, she had gone away. Because he was only a child the adults around him chose to keep the reasons, even the fact, of it from him, to protect him. All the child felt was the rejection of the person whose sole job was to enable him to feel trust and love.

'We don't have to go to any of those places?'

'Not if you don't want to. I am not going to make you do anything you do not want to do. You can trust me.' He put his toe in the water with this word. 'You can tell me at any time what you want to do and I will do it.'

'So we don't even have to get off the train?'

'Is that how you feel? You would rather not get off the train? Because if that is how you feel we will not get off.'

The child mused over this. This was new. He had been used to being told, not being asked. This made him feel different. He didn't know.

'I don't know,' he said.

The man looked out of the window, noting how the surrounding area was becoming increasingly bleak. Corrugated railway sheds abutted weed-infested sidings where rusting lines lay behind a gauze of green made sopping wet by the spring rain. He knew these were the signs they were drawing close to their first destination, but it seemed less urgent somehow. The excitement of his first meeting of the day had gone. He was feeling closer to the centre of his personal peace than he could remember. The last six months of agony, blaming, abandoning the trust he had built, believing it would be gone if he ever returned for it, had left him drained but somehow fortified.

He noticed that they were now alone in the carriage. This was the strangest thing. He could not recall this train being so empty before. He also had no idea when everyone else had got off.

'We can get off the train,' the child said.

'Are you sure?'

The child nodded. Suddenly he felt the need to mark out his new territory.

'But we can go back whenever I want?'

'Yes,' said the man. 'Whenever you say we can go home. You have my word.'

The train slunk into the station two minutes early. It announced itself with a couple of self-congratulatory jerks as it pulled up alongside the platform.

A guard in a peaked cap turned his black plastic whistle in his hand as he watched the carriages empty. He saw a solitary man leave the carriage with the poetry by Simon. His unconscious remarked to itself how unlikely it was that this man would be the only traveller in this carriage at a peak time of day. His conscious walked him over to the carriage and he looked in. It was empty.

He blew his whistle. It made a satisfactory peep. He waved his arm and the doors closed as if he were a magician. The train returned home.

The Therapist

She paraded before them lined up like chocolate soldiers dressed in their multicoloured all-weather jackets. 'Just Got Bigger' competed with 'Great New Taste', making choice more difficult than she remembered. Before, it had always been a surgical strike at the counter, emerging with a caramel centre in a no-nonsense milk chocolate outer, all encased in the kind of wrapping she could tear off without utilising the hand that cupped the mobile phone to her left ear as she raced her life between pit stops.

She couldn't remember the last time she had gone eye-to-eye with such temptation. There appeared to be two, three, four times the selection now. All the bars that had previously graced the shelves alone now roamed as part of an extended family embodying king-size, 20% extra and snack (and bite) attack. When had *that* happened? How could she possibly know the benefits of chunky over classic – was there a night class or Dummies' Guide she could turn to?

She looked around. Come to that, since when had motorway service stations become a destination shopping experience? How long had she been unaware of this? What kind of people dropped off the M4 and into these places to stock up on kettle descalent, onion gravy mix and the Demis Roussos Golden Collection? As she glanced down at the CD bearing the visage of that Greek god of plenty, she found herself standing next to a woman presumably wearing a pair of her husband's tracksuit bottoms which must have ill fitted them both. She was buying an illuminated lunar globe and a three-pack of popsocks bearing the Union flag.

'Any petrol?' the till operator asked this woman.

The tracksuit-bottomed customer looked at her askance and shook her head, as if this was an odd thing to be asked at a garage. She placed some pine and lemon grass air-freshener beside the globe, completing a link sale that no customer service training course had ever written into a role play.

She watched this transaction, burdened with an experimental chocolate bar that threatened a 'Total Lime Onrush!', and caught a glimpse of herself in the security TV screen on the desk of the till operator. She saw someone who looked the age she would be admitting to in ten years, decked out in a severe dark pinstriped suit adorned only by a bright blue brooch that seemed oddly incongruent with her black and white image. She realised that the last time she had felt so self-aware, as well as conscious of the world about her, Demis had been turning down cake in favour of enhanced celebrity; before the marriage, before the kids, before her daughter had been taken from them all, before the career and the divorce; before she had made a Faustian pact in return for aggrandisement and the kind of success that could be measured by a fine entry in the *Legal 500*.

Her strange choice of confectionery was different to yester-day's and different again to the one she would make tomorrow at the same time. She paid, and almost had to stop middle-aged legs from skipping back to her tiny red car. She felt so alive, as if the shackles that had manacled her to her guilt and self-loathing lay beaten and broken in the petrol-swirled puddles of the forecourt.

'Find somewhere safe,' she had been told by her therapist.

Safe? Her eyebrows almost touched the peak of the severe fringe the hairdresser had cautioned her against in a courageous moment, receiving a glare in exchange that had stopped his scissors in mid-snip. In a service station car park? She actually thought to herself, how is it possible even to be safe in a world that can snatch little girls from you with no warning?

Her therapist's instructions were clear. 'Pull up under the lights, grab yourself a treat, a chocolate bar, some flapjack, maybe even an alcopop, and lock yourself in. Turn off your phone and the radio and confine any kind of voice recording or electronic diarising equipment to the glove compartment.'

She had snorted. It was her 'claptrap code'; the kind of noise people like her were supposed to make with psychotherapists. It confirmed to her (her id, psyche, ego?) and anyone within range that she had little faith in the proceedings she longed to trust. But she still bought the chocolate. Flapjack was not for her. It was hydrogenated toxin, and she had always hated the taste of chemically excited raspberries.

'And then I have to sit and make this list?'

Her therapist had sat opposite her, gently cross-legged and serene in pastel cotton, smiling again. She didn't reply; somehow her patient had known she wouldn't.

'Can't I just think about this as I drive along? Christ, I'll be late enough home as it is.'

The smile again, but it was her session, she was paying for it and she continued her cross-examination.

'I have to sit for ten minutes in my car and make a list of all the things I have done that day I am proud of.'

'Or thought.'

'Or thought.'

In any other kind of meeting she would conduct during the course of her life, the soundlessness that followed would be considered a stand-off. That she could handle. She could squeeze a negotiating silence until it screamed, before launching her counterattack. Those rules of engagement did not apply here in this softly furnished room, where large, welcoming chairs with arms stretching out to comfort those who needed it blended with linen-hued dado-height wooden panelling.

There were black and white photographs on the walls of lakes and rolling plains etched with trees and scattered under limitless skies that did not need the words of Donald Justice to be scribed on them to whisper their peace. On a table by a sofa drowning under Indian patchwork cushions, a grand glass vase of a thousand white Asian lilies intoxicated the room with their scent. Scattered golden pollen spotted an oaken leather coaster on which the vase stood. She had been aching to blow that away, and onto the floor, from the moment she walked into the room for this session, her first.

'I think I will feel weird. You know, sitting in my car, alone, writing down things that I am proud of about myself. It makes me feel like a…'

The legs uncrossed and the tan Kurt Geiger court shoes met together as the woman stretched forward to hear what her patient would feel like.

'You know.'

'Well, I think I know what you would feel like. I am just unclear if you do.'

'Well, a little like a homeopathic fruiterian freethinker, if you know what I mean.'

'Frankly, no,' the therapist leant forward. 'You see, this is the point. I do not think you can possibly know what you will feel like when you do this, principally because I do not think you know who you really are. As I explained to you, this exercise is designed to bring those thoughts from the unconscious mind and introduce them to your conscious, reasoning senses.'

'I suppose you know best in this.' The patient felt herself seek the farthest reaches of her armchair. Only the cushion prevented her from sliding down the back, slipping past the lilies and out into the garden that tapped against the window behind where she sat.

'Certainly if I am ever in need of excellent commercial litigation advice I will come to you.' The therapist smiled again.

'I am curious,' she continued, 'who exactly is it you will be feeling weird or uncomfortable in front of? We have agreed that the things you write will belong to you and nobody else. We have also agreed you will tell no one you are doing this exercise and not show anyone what you have written.'

'I will feel strange in front of... myself.'

'Then it is this person we need to introduce you to. The person who has told me in the last forty-five minutes...' Here she consulted the notes her patient had not seen her make. She slipped a pair of frameless and seemingly lensless tiny glasses onto her nose as she read... 'that she is a dreadful mother of two teenage sons, a bad listener, an inadequate communicator, a flawed lawyer and a person, here I am quoting, "who does not blame her daughter for dying and her husband for leaving her".'

She looked up from the pad on her lap. The patient blinked at her, mostly because everything south of her eyelids felt frozen in place.

'This is a person we have to talk and listen to, don't you agree?'

Her patient nodded. Part of her wanted to stick out her tongue and run around this perfect room tipping things over. The self-control she had perfected and made legendary at the firm, as well as among people she occasionally called friends, was another conversation away.

'You have dealt with all this so well,' one of these friends had said, 'I would have gone crazy.'

Crazy? she had thought. What about the times she imagined herself being swallowed up by blackness; the nights she screamed into her pillow until her throat became raw? The silent screaming for fear of waking her sons, who already lay awake in their rooms listening out for their mother's sobs. What about the mornings she had to throw herself out of bed just to start the day, or the times she became jealous of her lost husband lying in hospital close to death? Jealous because she knew he was less crazy than her.

Crazy enough now to finally see a therapist who wanted her to make lists in car parks. Is that crazy enough for you? Still, she was mad enough to do as she was told. Having returned early from the training course, with the words of a poet still ringing in her ears, she made a pact with herself that she was determined to follow through. She deserved a future; another chance. If therapy could do what Norpramin couldn't, she was committed to giving it everything she had.

On the first occasion she had stopped at the agreed service station it was the little girl in her who had walked into the shop and begrudgingly bought a caramel bar, stomped back to her car and thrown her deactivated phone onto the passenger seat. She had stared at the new notebook, its spine creasing and crackling as it curled back on itself for the first time, waiting for something to happen.

It had been a lousy day. She could write screeds about the things that had gone wrong and about which she was berating herself. This would have followed the pattern of every other night she fought her way home after a ten-hour day, before the bickering campaign of mealtime with the boys began. She had told her therapist about these journeys. The blackness that could not be pierced by a million bi-xenon headlights; the self-doubt, the admonishment, the regrets all bound up and recorded in a timesheet she would charge to clients. Her language motif always followed the same shape. It would unfold and multiply as she unloaded the day into her head, confirming her fears, corroborating them.

She had promised she would spend ten minutes (definitely no more) focusing on the events that had made her 'proud' today. What a word. Why not simply 'good' or 'positive'? It had been thirty-two years since she had tussled with algebra homework, or fulminated against the fascination her headmaster had with the verbs in Esperanto. But this was harder. What was she 'proud of' today?

On that first night she had written down two things as she watched the clock on the dash of the car tick away the minutes. After exactly ten had passed she closed the book and continued her drive home to argue about pizza and mobile phone usage with the sons who were growing too much like the father who had left them all, at first to be with his grief and then with that woman…

The second night had been worse. On the third she wrote down three fragmented sentences, with a pre-dawn realisation that these things need not record memories of great inventions or significant breakthroughs; they could be moments in her day when she emerged from herself and did the things she would feel good about had they been done to her.

That made it a little worse. The therapist told her that, having accomplished a list, she should then spend some time evaluating the things she wrote, grading them and placing them in a descending order of pride. This, she was assured, would enable her cognitive senses to distinguish between useful and negative feelings, putting them in a place where she could assess them, plucking them from the shadows of her unconscious where they lurked in fear and reservation.

Now, back in the perfect room, the lilies breathing their perfume over soft furnishings swathed in cool ivory Alcantara, the therapist held up three fingers adorned with clear-polished pared nails. My God, woman, she had thought, you're an apparition! Haven't you ever fought with the handle of a full filing cabinet or snagged a nail on a sticky handbag clasp? I bet you bought your beautiful and overachieving children at 'Organic Fresh and Wild'.

This apparition of a woman spoke. 'It takes three weeks to make a new habit and three months to keep it. See this as your chance. The chance to take back control over your thoughts, and so your life. Your chance to change the habits of the last...' she scrutinised her patient, slicing through her defences; the business make-up and Akris suit... 'forty-six or so years.'

Bitch, she had thought, dead right.

'It is bound to feel strange at first. You are swimming against the tide of your internal script. This has been written throughout your life, scrolling the foundations of your negativity. Your inner voice will tell you that this is nonsense, useless; that you are who you are, a saved programme, full jug, signed painting. This is why it is so crucial to write these things down, show yourself how unreasonable you are being with yourself. How inaccurate your thoughts are.'

'Hardly rocket science,' she had both thought and said. The curmudgeon sitting before this therapeutic model of perfection had grumpily sought to tease a quarry who refused to even recognise the existence of bait.

'I am sure that rockets existed fruitlessly in the minds of many a dreamer until the day someone decided to commit their dreams to paper and make them real. The discipline of cognitive therapy makes it absolutely clear that it is the commitment of thoughts to writing that enables the thinker to turn a corner in their lives. Trust me, write it down – if only to come back and prove me wrong.'

On the fourth day of her service station regime she remembered nine or ten things that highlighted her day and on which she could give herself positive feedback. She had mentally noted two or three of these as they occurred: during a difficult meeting, in a queue that morning with a woman and her wretched screaming baby, the choice she had made not to bawl out a weird young girl in an electronics shop who appeared incapable of forming a sentence, let alone a decision on the return of goods. All times she pushed her pause button and chose a different decision; a greater part of herself.

In the car that fourth night she had chewed an experimental bilberry flavoured chocolate bar that had tingled in her mouth as she gunned down the first of these points into the notebook. Having completed the first part of her task and ranked the comments on the page in front of her, she barely noticed that the critical voices in her head had become quieter.

That night, as she indicated to rejoin the motorway, her thoughts became still, and for the first time she could remember noticing the edges of dusk touching the bare branches of trees that stood watching her and her fellow travellers from their vantage point on a noise bund protecting a housing estate from the worst roar of the traffic. That night she had watched the corners of her youngest son's mouth moisten as he laughed with her and his brother, recounting an incident from school. She did not, and never would, know that he would always recall the fact that this was the first time since his father left he could remember Mum laughing with him and his brother, an occasion that doubled in significance as he noticed she had no pile of papers beside her for company at the table.

There had been so many years and so much pain for him, for all of them. The death of his sister, his father's disappearance, the agony of rejection, then the misery of seeing him in hospital, bandages wrapped tight around his wrist. He saw his mother turning to work and self-denigration in order to cope, and finally his father's re-emergence with a new wife and sister that seemed, at last, to bring his mother to her knees.

Beyond this moment, on night five and for the week that followed, she had stopped her car in the same place and, by Tuesday, had celebrated the opening exchanges in her relationship with the cashier at till three by trading raised eyebrows over the shoulder of a mountain of a man who could not decide on the lottery scratch cards he would choose to take back to his car and leave untouched in the driver's door pocket.

That Friday she had sat for fifteen minutes scribbling furiously in the book and debating with herself the order of worthiness of her feelings of pride. It was something that, by stealth, entered her agenda of thoughts during the day. She found herself subliminally planning the words she would use and the order she would place them in. She forgot to unload the filthy laundry of her self-recrimination into the car as she drove to her slip road off the motorway and into the service station haven, too keen was she to make the most of this time with herself.

That Saturday she made an excuse to leave early from a friend's soirée and discovered herself driving back up the motorway. She acknowledged the apparent insanity of her actions. Surely, a sofa, a bench, even a bar stool would do just as well. But she was an intern in the college of self-awareness and did not dare to question the wonder of what she was discovering in herself. Like a salmon she was magnetically attracted to return to the place of her rebirth.

She found the junction that would enable her to reverse her journey back in the other direction, then up the slip road and into the service station. She discovered there was a weekend staff in the shop who she did not recognise and who would not know this woman with the strange habit of parking up and writing in a book while, with a new-found fickleness, choosing and devouring randomly selected chocolate bars. But that didn't matter; there were things she needed to write about this Saturday, the best she had spent with herself and the boys for as long as she could recollect. The list took more than twenty minutes to compose that night and she graduated from classic to chunky in her choice of confectionery.

Back in the pale room of personal reflection she recounted this incident. 'It's amazing. I seem to have forgotten how to think in a negative way about myself. I mean, it's been little more than three weeks but I feel, you know…'

She was perched on the edge of the Alcantara, bouncing her hands on her knees; the birds of paradise flowers that had played tag with the lilies, and now occupied the vase, bent forward to share her eagerness and catch her words. She felt herself reflected if not literally then figuratively in the eyes of the therapist, but her words still refused at the final hurdle.

'Actually, I think I do know. But do *you*?'

It was then she felt it. It had been part of the room when she had arrived for her first appointment. The feeling skulked around its periphery, poked its head through the bookshelves bedecked with glossy tomes and eerie wire-frame installation art, and captured the calm others sometimes felt as they walked out of their own sessions, back to their lives. There was a sense of peace she knew she could access for herself.

'I think I do.'

Her therapist held up the three fingers again. Could that possibly have been a chip in the nail varnish she saw? Could it have been an accident that a lock of white blonde hair fell across her forehead at that moment? My God, was that *dandruff*?

'I know, I know. It takes three weeks to make a new habit. It's been four with me, and I *love* it.'

'It will take three months for it to become part of your life. The sense of novelty will pass and then you will have to dig in and fight for what you most want. Behavioural change is about learning new habits and exploring their consequences. But most of all it is about graft and a will to want it when it is easier to give in. You will need to be relentless in the pursuit of this.'

'No, I *want* this. I had no idea what inner peace could be derived from taking control of your own thinking. I was wrong and you were right, it was the writing down and the evaluation of thoughts that made all the difference. There is no way I am letting this go.'

'Those old habits may have been forty-six years old, but this new one is much better than just being new. It is me, the me I have never known. Thank you.'

There was no miracle here, she knew that much. Her daughter was still dead and her marriage still over. But she had found herself in that notebook and was starting the steady climb back up the black hole she had not dreamed about for four weeks.

The therapist looked at a clock behind her patient.

'That's about it for today. I will see you again in another three weeks. I want to catch you before you get round to the caramel bar again.'

They both got up and the therapist offered her a hand. She shook it and made her way to the door.

'By the way, that is a beautiful brooch. Is it new?'

'It belonged to my mother. It *is* beautiful, isn't it?'

They both stood and surveyed the silence between them for a while. The woman then turned and walked out to her car. She decided to take the motorway home.

'To be honest, I can't see any problem with feeling a little miserable every now and again. It's normal isn't it?'

The therapist crossed her legs again. He noticed she was wearing the same combination of smart shoes and shimmering stockings that accentuated slim, well-defined calves. For some bizarre reason the image of her playing hockey entered his mind, although he thought a vigorous bully off would probably snap her in two.

'Absolutely normal, healthy and appropriate even. Why would you even ask the question?'

He looked at her, puzzled. He had never had this kind of conversation before. Was this what his ex-wife had craved of him? Wasn't it enough to win the Lotto and stop using hair gel? He followed her down what he thought may have been another of her verbal traps.

'It wasn't me, it was you. You said… something about my rational self seeking positive solutions.'

She slightly furrowed her brow, nibbled on the end of a slim silver pencil and consulted notes he was sure she didn't need. He was aware of the faint ticking of a clock he couldn't see as quiet suffused this pale unruffled room.

'Tell me about the "every now and again" part. How often is that?'

The nibbling stopped and she rested the pencil against her cheek in what he read as a pantomime parody of the question she had asked. Some insane flowers with absurd heads like velociraptors leaned in to listen to his answer. His rational self wasn't in the same street as the positive solutions he was supposed to seek out at the moment. He thought this self might be out getting pissed, looking through the bottom of a glass at irreverence and negativity as they shared a joke at his expense in the bar at the end of a dark corridor that had been his life after work for the last six months.

He rubbed a big hand up and down the arm of the chair. The

ginger hairs on his arms glistened slightly in the ambient light. In doing so he alternately excited and smoothed the nap of, what was this material, some kind of suede? Wasn't that for jackets and shoes that got scuffed by the edge of a brake pedal? He drew a circle with his finger, then rubbed it out with a sweeping motion of the soft underside of a fist. He used fingers of the same hand to randomly tap the material, mesmerised by them for a second as if not recognising why he should need such odd, dangly things.

'What exactly is it you want me to say here? I'm getting in touch with my feelings? The pain is becoming part of my life? Depression and I, we're two of a kind?' The ginger man exhaled heavily, looked up but avoided her gaze.

The only sound between them was the tapping of the sash window against its frame as an early afternoon breeze enquired as to the situation of its still air sibling within the room. This was the fourth time he had been here. On each occasion he had wanted to take his tools to the loose window fittings and fix them for her. That's what he could do: fix things, put up brackets, clean a set of alloy wheels until they hummed with joy, organise a sales' convention. Why couldn't she ask him to do this? Why wasn't that better than all this thinking?

The woman smiled. Not so much as to make him want to hurl one of those freaky see-through wire faces at her. Not a smirk; it was a smile that told him he had to work harder. That she expected more of him.

'How often?' she said.

'It's not getting better It's getting worse,' he answered. 'It's crazy, it's hopeless.' A pause longer than the blank moment of his mind. '*I'm* hopeless.'

She let the words hang there for a therapist's minute. 'Did you make your notes?' she asked him.

He sensed the folded wad of paper in the back pocket of his jeans, pressing against him. He could imagine some of the words imprinting on his buttock. He could unwittingly shower down at the gym tonight with words like 'hopeless' and 'loser' emblazoned across his backside. Glancing across at the flowers in the vase one of them seemed to nod. He told her he had made a few notes, but that they weren't much good. This wasn't his type of thing;

putting his feelings onto a piece of paper and then analysing them. He had decided to do them at the bar one time, but found he couldn't concentrate.

She smiled again. He took the sheets of paper from his pocket and uncreased them against his knee. He reached further in to retrieve a stubby little pencil. Ironic, wasn't it? He could now afford anything he wanted, but still liked the feel of a chewed pencil butt complete with yellow paint flaking from moist, splintered wood and sticking to his tongue.

'What do you want me to read out?'

She raised what had once been one eyebrow, but was now a perfect, thin arc of blonde hair. Come on, the eyebrow said, you know better than that. How long have you been coming here? He cleared his throat and made a circle in the suede with one of the fingers of his right hand.

When the words came out they sounded squeaky and unnatural to him. It was like telling the class about his history project again, the bit about the finding of the tomb in Egypt.

'This is shit. Everything is shit. Shit, shit, shit,' he read. He looked up at her. 'It's a work in progress,' he explained.

'I'm getting the picture,' she replied. The smile (work harder). He read on.

'I don't blame her for dumping me. She thinks I am a loser and she has a point.' He was almost wheezing with the effort now. He looked up. She waited. He bit on the end of his pencil and could taste the mixture of wood and graphite moistening in his mouth.

'This is what I am useless at. Making connection. There is nothing she or anyone else can connect with.' He stopped reading. 'Then I crossed some stuff out. I was rambling a bit, not making any sense.'

'What did you then do with those words?' she asked him. He regressed again.

'What happened at the tomb?' his teacher had asked him. 'What do you think Carter felt when he first broke through into the main chamber?'

He didn't know. It was a long time before. How could he know what a man who had died before his mum was born had felt about something? The older version of the schoolboy who had agonised over this now wondered how he could be expected to analyse thoughts that, as far as he could remember, had always been a part of him. This was the inner child she was helping him to 'get in touch with'.

He knew she had told him to write down in a personal log an event that had upset him. She had shown him how this should look. It was useful only if it was specific. Words like 'loser', whether tattooed to his backside or said out loud, were not bedmates of the process she was dragging him through. She did that weird thing she and others of her species had done before by piercing his protective ring of carefully nurtured 'man thoughts' and getting to the soft underflesh of feelings that cowered beneath.

'What specific event did you write in your log?'

'You say "specific"?' he asked. You say tomato, I don't, he thought. Let's call the whole thing off.

'Do you have your log there?'

He nodded. He had done his homework – sort of. Just as, twenty-eight years ago, he had drawn the outline of the magical death mask and some scarab beetles, but hadn't completed the essay on the team of tomb finders. He had known at the time that his feelings weren't 'specific' enough.

'How do you feel about reading that part of it out to me?'

What chance a meteorite strike right now? Could he get to the door without being taken down by a perfect extended calf? There was only one of him. He couldn't create a distraction. Instead he cleared his throat to minimise any squeaking.

'I've just told you.' He looked up at her, confused.

'Can I read the words back to you?' she asked him.

She had the words in the order he had said them but, as she repeated them to him, they sounded different without his stertorous punctuation. When she finished he decided to bluff it out, mocking her raised eyebrow as if expecting her to recognise the completeness of his sentiments.

This wasn't her first time, however. Her eyebrow raised higher and more confidently than his, and in seconds he caved in.

'What's wrong with that?' he squeaked. 'That is how I felt.'

'In this room we only deal with real problems. What you have described is a mirage of feelings. You are a loser, you cannot connect. You feel shit, shit, shit.

'You cannot deal with that because there is nothing to deal with. You say that you don't blame her for dumping you?'

He nodded again.

'Let's go there. Think of a situation where you remember feeling this. If you cannot recall the feeling, just describe what you were doing when you felt it. Where were you? What were you doing? What was the consequence of feeling it?'

He remembered returning to the airport in Antigua. He described to her the hollow feeling at the pit of his stomach that was about far more than the fact he had repeatedly thrown most of its contents down the head of the *Vita Da Sogno*. He could not face the First Class lounge and could not face the compact little airside shops selling watercolour beach scenes and dried flowers bound up like holiday wreaths. He could not face another moment on this claustrophobic archipelago and could not countenance a return to the UK with its pointless commuting and endless meetings.

He remembered getting a ridiculous travel document case out of the hopelessly effete brown holdall with fussy motifs she had made him buy at Heathrow. In there was a ticket she would never use. It had the words 'Return Open' printed on it, but the matter, she had assured him, was utterly closed. To stop the emotions getting too close to the surface, he had sucked in the musty body odour that seemed to permeate all public buildings in the Caribbean and refused to look at it again.

He described this to this woman.

'She reached beside her and picked up a neat little leather container that lay on the top of an ordered pile on her desk. Within it, nestled perfectly in its expensive casing, were three big pens that could be used to write on big paper. She handed one of them to him and pointed at a huge pad on long metal legs in the corner of the room. Even this was cloaked in a leather front sheet that perfectly accessorised this suffocating room.'

'Under there is a flip chart pad. Take this pen and write a list of all the negative emotions you feel when recounting your return to the airport.'

He didn't want to get up. He had to go to the front of the class. They called him 'carrot brain' and 'deadhead-red' under their breath as he made his way to the blackboard. His shoes felt like stone as he walked across to the big pad. The leather cover seemed too heavy as he turned it over the top of the huge easel that held it.

Deadhead-red wrote; desperate, alone, embarrassed, pathetic, stupid and four or five more words. He stopped and looked at her. She was not returning his gaze, but was looking intently at the words he had written as if willing them to come to life. He finally wrote, in big red capital letters, 'FURIOUS'.

'I want you to give each of those a score,' she said. 'Write a number out of one hundred beside each of the words. A low number would be the least you could feel, and one hundred the most. This will help you to rank your feelings, get closer to a sense of personal truth. It will also show you that you may have been thinking in the past in an "all-or-nothing" type way.

'We can then deal with the feelings in order.'

He took up the pen again and listened to the clock. The words on the pad fused in front of his eyes. Seeing them there felt like catching first glimpse of an enemy he had known to be converging on the other side of the hill on which he camped. He felt rooted to the spot but knew it was time for the grown-up in him to take over. He placed a 50 beside the word 'embarrassed' and 75 against 'desperate'. He followed that with other numbers before focusing in on the word 'alone'. He knew she was watching him and realised that she was probably ahead of him with the numbers he was writing.

He moved forward and put '100' beside the word 'alone'. He wasn't as furious as he thought, but he felt very, very alone.

'Let's look at that word,' she said. 'I want you to write down a negative thought that goes along with the feeling that word induces. Turn to a clean sheet of paper; write it on there.'

He did as he was told and faced down the next sheet of paper. He wrote on it, 'I am alone. I will always be alone.' He stopped writing but did not turn to face her again. He waited for a minute, maybe more, before writing. 'Because no one wants me.' He turned to look at her again.

'Now I want you to judge how true those statements are. To do this you have to become your own observer; watch yourself, listen to your thoughts and assess them for veracity.

'Rate those statements for truth between one and one hundred. Use the same scale as before. How true are they in reality? Stand away from your need to overgeneralise. How much accuracy lies in those statements?'

He hated this but knew it had to be done. It was his ticket out of here and punishment for his lack of preparation. Twenty-eight years ago, it had been the same; he hadn't done his homework on the findings in the tomb and could smell a cocktail of mints and some sort of fruity perfume (was it pineapple?) as his teacher leaned across him to turn the pages of the book on his desk.

'How many of Carter's team went into the tomb with him? Why did they ignore the curse? What were they feeling?' He had drawn the bugs in his homework book, concentrating on the black jewels of their eyes. He had hoped it would be enough.

He looked back at the first part of the statement he had written. Was he alone? He felt alone, but was he actually alone? How many of his friends had surfaced since the lottery windfall? How many of them made him feel more lonely than when they had not called and invited him to a barbecue on the beach before his good news? There had been new women, were they for real, or gold-digging like everybody else? What about his family? There had been a few awkward attempts at mending fences in the last five years. How did that feel now?

He analysed all of this and finally gave this part of his statement a score of 60.

On to the next sentence. Did he think he would *always* be alone? Which part of him really believed this? Standing in this beige negative of a room with its black and white art and columns of books, he realised, for the first time, that this was not the way he really felt. Sure, he felt sad and sorry for himself and it had become the signature tune to so many of his conversations. But was it true? He gave it a 25.

Finally the words, 'no one wants me'. As a child when he had imagined the tomb a weak lamplight played on walls of the antechamber that had not been illuminated for 3,000 years. The map must have been wrong. This was the way to the centre. He was getting closer to the very heart of things. The feelings encircling him now were atavistic, part of everything.

'I can't mark that one.' He held the pen over the words on the flip chart, its capped nib wandering back and forth under them.

'Why not?'

'I know I shouldn't feel it…' He gulped and waited for the klaxon to sound and lights to flash, heralding a grand *faux pas*. He had used the 's' word. She said nothing. It was one of those conversations that he wished produced an electronic pause followed by an options screen. Press 'A' for self-destruction, 'B' for the sudden appearance of a time tunnel and the opportunity to return to the moment just before the statement, and 'C' for a ventriloquist's puppet to explain that, in fact, the statement had been made by someone else who was not presently in the room.

'That is a "should" statement, isn't it? I am not giving myself permission to feel something else. Isn't that it?' But the therapist wouldn't be drawn. She knew enough about moves to recognise the coming of the end of the dance.

'Place a number beside the statement on the chart, even if it is not the right one,' she persisted.

He wrote in 90, and made the 0 look like a 6, but at a push it could have been a 1.

'Let's look at the distortions in what you have just said. There is a huge amount of "all-or-nothing" thinking within the phrase "no one wants me". You have magnified the issue out of all proportion, labelled yourself unlovable and blamed it on yourself.'

'And all before tea,' he said. Having escaped his mouth, the flippancy darted around the room and found a place to hide behind a row of books dedicated to revealing true meaning in communication. She ignored it.

'Should we work on a statement that is more rational? We are not looking for phoney truths here, but something closer to reality.'

'OK, OK. *She* doesn't want me.'

'Is she "everyone"?'

'At times she felt like it.'

'Really?' She leaned forward in a way he had learned was always a precursor to challenge. 'So this person who was every-thing to you was the woman you ignored for large periods of time, fell out of love with and spent time drinking to avoid? Look, I am not trying to deny you have issues, but at the same time it does not serve you to feed your automatic thoughts that are laden with untruths.'

She waited a moment before continuing.

'If you were to replace the phrase "because no one wants me" with a more rational response, what might it be?'

'She didn't want me.'

'And so you are alone?'

'Yes.'

She tapped the silver pencil against her cheek again. He sat down.

'So if we were to replace the statements you made before could we say, "I feel lonely at the moment because my wife has chosen to be with someone else"…'

'Yes.'

'And how would you score that – for truth?'

'100, or at least 95, I suppose.'

'Would your 5 look like a 6 or a 2?'

'More like an 8.'

'OK,' she said.

She was a little surprised and used a thinking pause to hide this reaction. He had responded much better to cognitive therapy than she had predicted. Her next goal would be to get him to write down this sequence of rationalisation without the need for her help.

She looked at the clock above his head. There were still ten minutes before his session ended.

'Can we try something?' she asked him.

What – with only two minutes or so to go? he thought. He was mulling over the likelihood of chicken nuggets and brown sauce. Carrot brain had earned his tea tonight.

'I would like to do a little role play,' she said. 'You play you, and respond to what I say as honestly as you can. Later you can write down your answers and rank them for truthfulness.'

It sounds dreadful, he thought. 'Great,' he said. That would be a 3, he thought.

'I am going to work with you to recognise there can be shades of grey in the way you internally process information. After you say something I want you to estimate then state aloud a number that represents the level of truthfulness of your words as you say them. This will get you used to the idea of ranking these automatic thoughts.' She paused.

'You say your wife…'

'Ex-wife,' he corrected.

'*Ex*-wife?'

'There's a decree absolute waiting unopened on my kitchen table,' he said.

'You can *sense* this?'

'The envelope has been lying unopened there for the last two weeks. I've been using it as a coaster.'

She nodded. 'You say your *ex*-wife dumped you because you were a loser, and you can see her point?'

'Yes.'

'And you are alone because no one wants you?'

'Yes,' he said. He thought about ranking that statement out of 100. How true was it? Was he really alone because no one wanted him? 75, possibly 70, he thought.

'Have you always been a loser?'

'Probably.'

'I have always been a loser. Rank that one out of 100 for me.'

He thought of the time he had won the hockey trophy. He remembered a house medal at school – long jump, wasn't it? Or spelling. He thought of helping his mother into the car from her wheelchair and remembered her face as he did it. She took everything with such grace, his mother. And she really loved him. He thought about the time he had rushed back from that cursed meeting in Scarborough to see her in hospital. He had virtually had to bribe the ward sister when he turned up more than an hour after chucking out time. He saw the light on his mother's face as he put his head around the door. She said she had never been happier than to see him there. He was with her when she died two hours later.

He remembered his wife throwing back her head and laughing in a restaurant at a story he had told. Other diners turned and stared, some of them starting to giggle themselves as they watched this wonderful woman hurling herself at her life, unabashed by her circumstances and unhurried by a waiter living his job title by holding a sorbet for her, a comma in the page of menu degustation they were working their way through. They made love in the car that night and she told him she loved him.

He remembered that bloke from *The Bill*, the one with the scar, handing him an oversized cheque, the word 'Lotto' big enough to be seen by every camera in the room. 'You're a winner,' the bloke had told him.

'30, maybe, 40.'

'You were smiling before you said that,' she said.

'Possibly 20 – feels like more.'

'So how do you reconcile this with the fact that no one wants you, and no one ever will? You haven't been perfect and you and your ex-wife failed to save your marriage, but that doesn't make you a loser. It makes you a divorcee.

'Is it possible that your ex-wife was at all to blame for the end of your marriage?'

'She screwed a Scottish boat designer on holiday while I was dying on board a yacht. I would say there was some blame there.'

'How about before? Before the win, before the holiday. Would you say that she was in any way responsible for the way your relationship changed?'

'You can't pin this on her.'

She leaned forward again. She pointed at him with the pencil. She tapped him on the knee; it was the first physical contact they had ever made with each other.

'Think about it again,' she said. 'In your estimation, looking back over the events before the holiday, do you think your ex-wife has any degree of responsibility for the breakdown of the relationship between you?'

He struggled against it but finally came up with an answer.

'Some,' he said.

'How much?'

'You want a number from me?'

She looked at him, eyebrow raised. How much attention have you been paying to the last thirty minutes? it asked him.

'14, 90, 210.6. What does it matter? The fact is she left me and I'm miserable.'

She persisted. 'How much responsibility are you giving your ex-wife for the way your relationship deteriorated? 100 means it was all completely your fault. Come on, take the pen and write that number down on the pad for me.'

He got up again and made his way past the velociraptors to the pad. The carpet felt soft against his shoes. He had never noticed how soft the carpet felt before. He wrote a number on the flip chart. She looked at what he had written and checked it against something in her notes. Had she predicted this? How close was she?

'Now,' she said, 'rank, for me, your level of misery before you went away with her for the last time, before the win, before you even bought that ticket. Put a number to that. How miserable were you, out of 100, before that time?'

He didn't want to. His head hurt. He wasn't enjoying this game. But she wasn't leaving it alone, both of them had a sense that there was something happening here, but only she had any clue where it might lead.

'What?' he said. She waited. He continued. 'I have been miserable for a long time.'

'As miserable when you were with her as you are now she has gone?'

He looked at her. What was this? Why was she doing this? He nodded.

'How miserable? Put a number to it. Compare the feeling before she left with the feeling now. Is it bigger, smaller, about the same?'

'Smaller.' He paused; there was no chance of this going away. 'But not much smaller.'

'Give me two numbers so I can compare the two feelings. One for your unhappiness when she was in your life, and another for now she is no longer with you.'

'60... 90.'

She sat back. He recognised that it was not for her to think about these numbers, but for him. The tick of the clock behind him seemed to slow.

'I want you to think about that relationship as it was then. Really focus on it. I want you to think about all the other relationships, of any sort, you have had in your life before then. How many of them would you rank as successful?'

He drew lines with his finger on the arm of his chair.

'This wasn't all her fault. You can't just pin it all on her.'

'Think about other relationships. Friends, colleagues, women, family. Were they all unsuccessful?'

He looked up at her. He could see her now. She had hidden behind her words and her fancy black and white photographs before. He shook his head.

'Give me a number.' Her voice softened and became very quiet. 'A number that says how successful other relationships in your life have been.'

A voice in the room said, '60.'

'That is not the number of a loser,' she said. 'Did any of those people want you? As a friend, a man, confidant, lover?'

'Some of them,' he said.

'More or less than 60%?'

'More or less,' he answered her.

She looked at the clock. She had broken a rule for him. They were seven minutes over time. Her next patient would be arriving soon, could even be waiting for her, adorned by that beautiful brooch, her tiny red car parked outside.

'Before next week I want you to think of all those people and write down their names in your book. I want you then to place two numbers by each of their names. The first one represents how much they wanted you, in the context of your relationship with them, and the other one should rank the success of the relationship.

'Bring your thoughts with you when you see me next time. I would like to talk about that.'

He rose from his chair, slightly bewildered. He wanted to say something to her as he walked past her to the door. He didn't know what it was. She smiled at him again. He walked into the room's waiting area, its own antechamber, only a secret to those outside who did not know what went on in this ordinary suburban house.

There was a woman sitting on one of the two comfortable chairs flicking through one of the magazines on nutrition and well-being that were scattered across the table between the chairs.

They exchanged looks that betrayed their shock at catching each other there. She had always known him as her husband's friend, but knew nothing of his recent history, apart from sharing one recent journey on a commuter train. To her he seemed different, softer somehow. To him her new vulnerability only added to her allure.

'Hello,' she said, first to recover.

There was something about discovering each other in this place that came to the assistance of the equanimity of the moment.

'I think I have warmed her up for you. Watch out for the flowers; they're killers this week.' He smiled at her in a way he had always wanted to, but had never known how. To his surprise she smiled back. He had always thought that she had an after-burner intellect and temper to match. His wife never felt comfortable in her company and they had rarely seen each other as a four. But here, now, they were down to two.

'How is…?' She had forgotten his wife's name.

'She isn't,' he said. 'Not dead or anything; she's just one of the entries on my list now.' He nodded towards the room he had left and she was about to enter. She smiled again, warmer than before.

'How are you?' he asked. He really wanted to know. He wanted to tell her that he really didn't know; that he hadn't seen her husband recently and that he wanted to talk to her. It never crossed his mind to tell her he was rich now.

'Better,' she said. 'The boys are good. Do you like football?' How strange, she thought. Why had she asked him that? They talked for two more minutes, filling in the easy clues of their crossword. 16 across – a chance meeting with the hope of something more. 11 letters; something, something, double s… could he see her again?

'I'll write my number down for you and leave it out here.' He pointed at the table she had been sitting at, spotting the therapist in his mind's eye standing by the door.

'Have you done your homework?' he asked.

She got a ream of lists out of her handbag and waved them at him. They laughed together.

'Can I photocopy them for my session next week? Could I maybe see you? Would next week be good?' he asked her.

'Next week will be fine,' she said, and thought that it really could be.

The Author

'I don't get it.'

He looked round at her, peering over his shoulder, frameless glasses suspended on the end of her nose. As he sat watching her for a second he saw her lips move over the words she was reading on the screen in front of them both.

'What don't you get?' His wife was always the first and last person he wanted to read his unpublished manuscripts.

'This path at the hospital, the one that leads to a broadening expanse of green, is it the same one that woman looks at as she sits on the wall? And if it is, does it mean she only pictures her escape through her madness? That's depressing.'

He was waiting to see if this was a question he was expected to answer. There had been many before, more than he could answer; more than he wanted to answer as he asked himself the same questions. He looked out of the window that watched over him at his desk. The sun was down, but he could still make out the shapes of conical spruce trees standing against each other as they fought for the horizon. Soon they would join together in an amorphous silhouette against the sky, before finally succumbing to the dark of a moonless October evening Closer to home, a lone street lamp held its amber flame captive, erect alongside the thick blackberry bushes that lined the road to the village.

She plonked herself down onto the edge of his desk, placing a stockinged foot on the armrest of his chair.

'So is the boundary the edge of her sanity? And where is she going? From madness to sanity, or in the opposite direction?' She was doing that thing with her hair. Forging ringlets with her fingers and letting them go, bouncing them off her shoulder blades and onto the soft blue cardigan whose too-large neckline fell down to reveal the flesh on her upper left arm. As her interrogatories increased in intensity he knew that she wanted an answer. It was always the women she identified with the most. Did she think they were based on her?

'I don't know,' he said simply. He watched her. They had been here before. She knew the rules and mostly kept to them. He placed his hand on her foot, gently squeezing her toes, feeling them through the sheer material, knowing their shape. Would she do it this time? Would she ask him questions she knew he wouldn't answer?

'What do you mean, you don't know? She's yours, you created her.'

'No,' he said, 'I didn't.'

Where had she come from, this woman on the wall? What were her secrets? How many people would ask him about her, demanding her antecedents, needing him to crack the mystery for them? She lived outside his brain, his fingertips, the keypad and hard drive. She was alive in the minds of people who gave her breath and shape, who took her with them down the path that led to the broadening expanse of green.

He felt no ownership, no responsibility. He could no more kill her than give her life at the beginning of her journey from city to pathway. He wasn't about to admit that he had also questioned her sanity as she sat on the wall with the figure who became a man as they faced the city.

The author had met her a number of times as he trawled the fertile waters of cities he visited. He saw her rushing through a department store, oblivious to herself and the havoc her over-loaded wheeled suitcase wreaked as it strove to keep pace with their progress. On that occasion she had shoulder-length chestnut hair framing nutmeg eyes and a nose too small, pert and down-turned to be found in other people's affairs.

He had once seen her on a train sporting a blonde bob, staring out of a dirt-streaked window at a weak sun that was struggling to rise above the sentry pylons that guarded the last remnants of night. She absently rolled her mobile phone over and over in her hand, occasionally checking the high resolution display for signs of life. Was she willing it to ring or dreading its call? They had sat diagonally apart in sidings, watching together the progress of a man wrapped in a coat, as if surprised by the first day of spring, trudging behind a ginger dog, its gleeful head careering at angles from a body barely able to hold it in the exhilaration of running anew across a field it had known all of its life.

He saw her looking out across the field to a group of houses huddled around steam that rose from their vents and chimneys to curl around trees that had relented in the last fight against a disappearing winter. Was this beautiful to her, or desperate? Was she on the train to leave somewhere, or return to it? There was something in her eyes as she looked past, through him, to track the flight of an arrow of geese as they returned home over the train which the two of them unwittingly shared. The eyes held something wild, with serenity in their outskirts.

He had seen her again with frenzied auburn hair and the intensity of steel in a supermarket, glancing surreptitiously at the contents of the trolley of two young men, comparing them with her own that she pushed up and down the ranks of shelves and deep freezers. For these men the aisles of the store were like a theme park, all jostling and laughter as they filled their cart with beer and mince, and their lives with adventure. The sadness of her then was revealed not only in her neat packaged meal for one, two florets of cauliflower and a low-fat apricot yoghurt, but in the way she rested her arms on the bar of the trolley it appeared she could not push a millimetre further. Not for her the 'Offer Of The Week' or the 'Price Fall Sensation!' Around the corner along from frozen foods. Down the aisle, past the check-out conveyors, into the car park and on to oblivion.

Having spotted her, he walked out of the supermarket and felt the chaos of the city they shared. He was sure he could hear her screaming over the rumble of traffic, and went home that night to pen her escape.

Write about something you know, he had been told. He was sure he knew this woman, in her many guises, careering robotically around the city in search of a wall to sit on. He was never certain who or what he would write about next, but knew she was in no way connected to the toes of the foot he was holding as they wriggled to his touch.

Five hours later it was dark outside with no movement on the road. His wife was back with him; their conversation had gone unfinished through the evening meal, unspoken questions garnished with untold answers. She now did that thing he would never understand. She read his thoughts and offered them to him.

'How do you know what to write next? Would it be the same if you went away and returned to it an hour later? What if we had gone out to the cinema the night you wrote about the path, and when you came home you had her return to the city and back to her life there? There's a lot of God in an author.'

He looked across at the shelves on the other side of the room they were in. There was a book on them he had read often.

'What was it Karl Jung said? When a man becomes truly evolved he becomes a woman.'

'You wish,' she said ruefully.

'No, no really. What is it you women always flaunt at us men, like it is the grail out of which we can never drink? You tease us with your tales of instinct and take it from us again by telling us we can never understand it. How many arguments have you won by explaining your position as "instinctive"?'

'What is it you are saying? That we are shallow and devious?'

'*God* yes,' he retorted, 'but not just that. That you are *right*. There's a part of us all that keeps our instincts in check, denies who we truly are and leads us back to what we and others expect of us.

'We men spend too much time blanking this part of ourselves, facing in the opposite direction, ignoring our greater side.'

He saw her reflection in the window he faced. She was regarding him and considering her response to this. They did not often do this together, talk about who he was when he wrote and how this made her feel. It was a fragile moment for them and he could tell they were both thinking of it like a chess game.

Knight to bishop four. Two moves to castle. If she said this, his queen may be endangered; how would he respond?

'So, you write only through instinct? How much of that is consciousness and how much is accident? Don't you feel that you have a greater responsibility to those who may read what you write and use your words to form the next part of their lives?'

He spotted the threat and placed his king behind a rook.

'More and more, through the characters in this book and a

greater awareness of life that has emerged in writing it, I have learnt to trust my instinct. A year ago I was producing character sketches, plot lines and treatments to trace the progress of the life that was surfacing through the pages I was writing. But this was killing the book, and murdering me.

'The greatest part of the adventure for me is the fact I have learnt to trust myself. And the more I trust the more trustworthy I have become. I can feel it expanding within me. I can sense my instincts growing, flooding my body and soul with energy.'

His breathing had become shallower now, as if he was saving the life force within him for something greater. He continued.

'Oh, and by the way, I have no responsibility for the thoughts and actions of those who may read this book. That belongs to them. It is neither something I want nor something they can give away. My full focus is on being the greatest I can be; once my words hit the page and stay there, that is where my responsibility to them ends.'

'Can't instincts be wrong?' As she said it he knew this was at the centre of her reservations.

So many words, so much to say. He glanced down at the keyboard in front of him. He wanted to write down this conversation and include it in a chapter, but knew he would be seriously endangering his relationship, and possibly his body parts, if he did this.

The headlights of a passing car briefly illuminated the corner of the lane on which their house stood. He saw the new gates they had saved for and erected together cast into light followed by instant shadow as it swept by. He had wanted grand and statesmanlike; she had wanted sympathetic and bucolic. Neither of them had won, but they had enjoyed the compromise.

'Not in their purest form,' he answered slowly. 'To my mind when we move away from the chatter in our heads and connect with the simplicity and purity that lives beneath, we go to a place where there is no need for the words "right" and "wrong". Our instincts take over like a generator that fires up when the lights go out.

'Also, even if the words I write do not, despite my best intentions, come from my instincts, I rely upon those of the reader to tell them about truth and lies. What do *their* instincts tell them? Is this a clue they can follow to help them write their own story? And if neither of us is working with our instincts, the biggest and best thing this tells us is that if we did something greater would happen.'

Enough, he thought. He turned round to look at her. She appeared impassive; she was staring at the moving collage of the screen saver behind which the words that had sparked this conversation lurked unseen.

'What if people cannot find their clues? What if this scares them and makes them feel lonely? What if all their instincts tell them is that they are alone?'

He became aware that he was drawing light circles on the underside of her foot with his finger. He felt her leg tense and did not know whether this was to a reflex motion caused by his inadvertent tickling, or the torsion transmitted by her thoughts.

He didn't want to answer too quickly, thus appearing to make light of her question. He looked at the green light of the digital clock in order to count at least three beats of the electric colon before he replied. It was forty minutes before midnight. He only made it as far as two beats.

'They would need to ask themselves if they were certain of the voice to which they were listening. Then they should ask themselves a different question, one that enabled their instinct to feel free to respond.'

She frowned. His wife, he knew, was a gentle childlike person capable of wondrous moments of adult behaviour. She could be mischievous and fun, creating as well as capturing the spirit of life in those around her. But there were shadows that chased her, demons she had never put to rest. More than anyone he had ever known this character combination enabled her to incisively cut through to the epicentre of a conversation. She did that now.

'Maybe these lonely people have forgotten what it is like to feel instinctive. Maybe it is all they can do to get through the day.' He knew it then, she was thinking about her sister and the baby.

'Maybe these lonely people need to do one thing each day, however small, to relearn about themselves and their instincts.' He looked at her as he said this. Her beautiful blue eyes, made softer by the colour of her cardigan, glistened in a moistness that was close to tears.

'What if they can't?' She said this so softly that the tiniest breeze against the bare branches of trees outside could have stolen the words away. But he heard them and squeezed her foot.

'Then they shouldn't do anything. They should wait for as long as it takes for things to change. Ultimately, this may be what their instinct is telling them to do.'

It had not always been this way for the author. He had not always trusted his instinct. He remembered once sitting on an uncomfortable stool in a coffee shop wondering about the lifespan of flecks of chocolate on top of his cappuccino. He placed the tip of his finger onto the foam and allowed some of them to stick to it.

'How long has it been now?'

His friend considered the question. Could he be regarded as a 'friend' if they only met twice a year, and was the likelihood of acquaintance increased by the fact that the person sitting opposite him had shared this intimate secret with him so many years ago?

'Six years next month.'

'Six years? How do you do it?'

'It becomes easier. She has no idea and has stopped asking any questions about, you know.'

'Why you're not having sex?'

'Oh, you *do* know.'

'Well, you have told me enough times. And she doesn't guess, you think?'

His friend shifted on his stool. There was a biscotti to attend to, and the ripping of Italian plastic wrapping was enough of a distraction for a man who wanted to make it so.

'Well, things have moved on a little.'

A woman dressed in sports trainers with soles as thin as pancakes asked if they wanted a stool that sat unoccupied more than four feet away from them. She had a slight squint in her eye, enough to slow the response of two men, who were unsure as to whom the question was directed. She took the stool and the author returned his gaze to his friend.

'In what way.'

'The kids know.'

The traffic that had been hurtling in both directions outside the window and the big city people who were filing past three deep on a pavement designed for two thin people all stopped, and everyone within two miles turned to look at the two men. The choking, gurgling coffee machine halted in mid-latte and a brown droplet froze on its spout. The woman with the squint took both of them in at once.

'How? *What?*' He spluttered, 'Why?' He was only a 'who' and 'when' away from the whole 'Inquisitor family'.

'My daughter must have read a text message from him on my phone. It wouldn't have been hard to interpret. She asked me about it and demanded an answer. At first I tried to make out that it was a spam text, a joke sent to me by a colleague, but she had already investigated further and printed off some emails from my laptop.'

'You kept emails? You didn't delete your texts?' Karl Jung in the corner of the coffee shop turned away from his elderberry tea and tutted in their direction. He knew there were no such things as accidents. His mate Freud attending to a skinny mocha a couple of seats away, on the other hand, blamed it all on someone's mother.

'No! How was I to know they would read my texts?'

'How old is your daughter again?'

His friend grunted and tapped a spoon against his cup.

'Fifteen,' he answered.

'And you think a fifteen-year-old girl wouldn't be interested in your mobile phone, do you? What about...?' How embarrassing, he couldn't remember his friend's son's name. Every time they met he promised himself he would write it down.

'Seventeen.'

'Do you know why they looked at your phone in the first place?'

'They didn't say. They said something about being suspicious, but I don't think they meant it.'

'What did you do?

His friend rocked the stool he was perched on gently backwards and forwards. Of course, he had known this line of questioning was bound to follow. He had invited it, so he could hardly get ratty and reject it when it turned up.

'I sat them down and we talked about it.' He looked at his friend, the rim of his cup shutting off everything from chin downwards. 'I told them everything. How I have been seeing him for six years, how hard that has been for me. Why I haven't told them or their mother before; everything.'

'How did they…? I mean, what did they *do*?'

'They cried. Well, we all did really. I think it helped.'

'Would you like to cry again now?'

'Would you like this biscuit rammed up your nose?'

The author had so many words, so much to say. He glanced down at the mug now only half filled with frothy coffee in front of him. This was another conversation he wanted to write down immediately. However, he realised that he was not here as a writer, but as a friend. In the last three months, with words lodging between his brain and his keyboard, he had found being an author hard. Now he realised that being a friend was harder.

'When was this?' he asked.

'Oh, about three months or so ago.'

Three months? People had fought and lost wars in that time, been diagnosed with cancer from what they thought was a healthy position and died. What had happened since the time father and children had sat around, talked and cried together? What of the mother, who was being sketched here as a character completely unaware of what the three most important people in her life were talking and crying about? He looked at his friend across the hapless little table in this standard high street coffee bar and raised his eyebrow in the non-verbal inquisition of a species who had spent so much time in recent generations analysing themselves. And? this eyebrow said. What happened next? What of the emotions that could have been used to surf out of the room where this talking and crying had taken place? What had they all done with them? What of the next conversation, the screaming and accusations? What of the denouement in the kitchen, late into the night, with knives glinting in blocks and pans sitting on shelves, aching to be thrown? What of the agony and the pain? What of the confessions and recriminations?

Nothing. His friend, content he had made the announcement he had been rehearsing on the Piccadilly Line all the way here, was thinking about the muffin he had very nearly bought at the front end of their meeting. He had offloaded the information that had been festering in him for three months and given it to this man, his friend, the author, in front of him. It would need time to settle for a while and they would perhaps talk about it some other time, if it needed talking about at all. He hadn't even noticed the eyebrow raised precariously against his friend's brow and wouldn't have realised what he was expected to do with it had he spotted it.

'And?' The eyebrow needed verbal assistance. It came in the guise of a three-letter word.

His friend was wondering whether the blueberry muffin was a healthier option than its choc-chip neighbour. Did he have to return to the counter and buy another coffee to lay claim to one? The word 'and' uttered, as it was, without pretext or noun entered his auditory filters and emerged triumphantly with an image of both muffin shaped objects of desire on a plate. Maybe they could share?

'*And?*' his friend repeated. 150,000 generations of communication between human beings enabled him to realise that this was a word that needed addressing. It was a question, albeit not a complete one.

'And?' he mimicked, searching for a hook to hang the question on. Of course, part of him knew precisely what the 'and' was attached to, it was just that his subconscious had decided it was best kept hidden until all other options had been exhausted.

The author was not to be deterred. 'What happened next, crud brain? What happened after you blurted this sordid truth out to your teenage kids?'

'Nothing, really. I promised them that it was going to be OK and that I wasn't about to leave their mother. I explained that I was taking no risks – physical risks, you know.' He raised his own eyebrow here, wanting his friend to nod his understanding without either of them having to put words into the conversation that had never been spoken between them.

His friend nodded, picking up on the elevated eyebrow and the need to nod to avoid the words he didn't want to hear.

'And?'

'And that's it. Nothing else has changed.'

'For you.'

'What?'

'Nothing has changed, for *you*.'

His friend nodded, baffled by this statement of what he thought was the obvious.

'But for your kids everything has changed. They now have knowledge of something that could change them and their lives for ever.'

That is when it did change for the author's friend. This is why, he supposed, he had arranged this meeting and rehearsed his lines on the tube. He had known that his friend would find the words he had been denying for so long. He had just hoped *these* wouldn't be the words he would find. His friend continued.

'What about your wife? What has she done with all this?'

His friend was appalled. These were definitely not the words he thought would be found here.

'She doesn't know. They haven't told her.'

The author thought it through. A fifteen-year-old daughter, close to her mother, keeps the counsel of a father she discovered at the end of a horrifying trail of suspicion has been cheating on them all with another man for six years.

'She knows,' he said.

His friend just looked at him, suspended in time.

'And you know she knows.'

His friend just shook his head. He closed his eyes and shook his head.

'No,' he said.

Something clicked here in the mind of the author. He had arrived at this meeting in the city, after a smoky lunchtime commute, a little reluctant to talk around the outskirts of issues he did not wholly understand with a man he did not fully empathise with. His wife had said he should go, he had been moping around his desk for two months now fighting with the chapter that would enable, at its conclusion, a confident man to talk to his inner child.

Why should he go? He wasn't even drinking coffee at the moment. He had been stuck on the book and searching for resolution. What would the man on the wall looking with him at the buildings of the metropolis have said? 'The person you think you are is perfect for the city. You can want, hope, wish (and search) for anything, but that person cannot walk down the path.'

Now he was here with his friend in a coffee bar in the city and he realised something.

'What does your instinct say about this?' he asked of his friend.

'What?'

'Come on, forget all of the excuses and rationality you have built as walls around you for a moment and look to your instinct. What is it saying to you?'

His friend shook his head, baffled by this new departure.

'I don't know,' he said. And he didn't. It had been so long since he had engaged any part of his instinct, he had no idea how to access it here.

'Then you need to look for clues,' he said. 'There must be clues. A raised head at the dinner table, or one kept firmly bent over a plate when something is said; an exchanged look in the middle of a conversation, or your wife fixing a stare on you in the bathroom mirror when she thought you were occupied cleaning your teeth. Clues. They will be all around you.

'The clues will feed your instinct and the more you rely upon that part of you the more you can tune into your life. Your instinct will know what to do.'

His friend shook his head again.

'She can't know,' he said.

'Look for the clues.'

They had shaken hands and promised to be in touch within the month. He knew they wouldn't, and that it would be another coffee shop after Christmas, but that was fine.

'Don't text me,' he said as his friend disappeared down the stairs leading to Green Park station.

The author turned away, wondering which way to take his thoughts, and saw the man again. Well, at least he thought it was him. It was always so hard to tell as one baseball cap pulled hard over the head of a cold, thin, white-faced London man looked pretty much like another. This time the man was leaning against some railings holding a magazine that looked almost too heavy for him. They may have made eye contact, but he could not see the man's eyes as they fell into the shadow of the brim of his hat.

He looked so cold and frail jammed there against the railings framed by the chateau like architecture of the Ritz Hotel, standing beneath one of the huge copper lions on the corner of the roof. It was then he decided to warm him up and place him on the decks of the *Vita Da Sogno*. Then, even if the sun didn't heat him sufficiently to give advice to a broken guest, at least he could listen. Would this be the same man who perched on a stool in the bar, listening to the wishes and dreams of a miserable ginger man who wouldn't find them until he learnt where to look? He wasn't the poet, reluctant or otherwise, and had probably never sat on a hill watching verdant fields tussle with marching conurbations. At least not yet. Maybe he too would be inspired by the words of that poet and find a small, crumbling hut somewhere that would enable him to gather the words together to save a man from himself before he made a journey into disaster. It would be a while before he saw an eagle rising on a thermal below him against the Colorado rocks, and he may never write a poem about it.

Could they be the same person? He knew he would be asked that too.

'Make it a little easier on people. Give them names, for God's sake. Can't they have a little identity, would that be so wrong?' his wife had asked him. At times her manner was so subtle as to be entirely invisible.

'They will have names. Just not the ones I choose to give them.'

He knew he shouldn't have his favourites, but the man in the cap was his. Although he knew he had been defensive in his response, he thought about what his wife had said. What would he call him? Ken? Ron? Why did he think he would possess a monosyllabic name? He had felt possessive about him from the start, and it was for this reason that he let him attend the course. Not to meet the poet; well, not only that. He thought he would get the most out of the course, that it would help him understand about the design.

Two years later, on the platform of a station, he would be cornered by a man who presumably recognised him from his picture on the inside back cover of the book. The man would take the book from a huge pocket stitched bizarrely down the side of an enormous flare adorning his khaki trouser leg, as if he always carried it like a reference work. Or a weapon.

He would remember wanting to be amused by being gesticulated at by a battered and bruised copy of his book, accessorised by stickers, tabs and marginal notes, but was actually quite disturbed by the intensity it would assume in this man's life.

He would think at first that this man wanted him to sign the book, but would soon realise this would never cross his mind. Far from being a chance meeting with a saviour or celebrity, it would be an interruption or embarrassment for a reader who had constructed a mental picture of the author that did not fit with the reality standing before him, somehow smaller and less heroic than the fictionalised version inside his mind. However, he would grab the opportunity.

'Why was he even on that course?' The author would suppose at the time it was a reasonable question to be asked, although the fact it was rattled off, as he looked for escape routes or a saviour of his own, as part of what seemed to be a prepared interrogation, was disarming.

'Surely this is not at all a place he would find himself in?' the man in the khaki flares would continue. 'What are you saying, exactly, that he works with all these other people, that it is a corporate thing? And if the woman in the antique blue diamond brooch is a lawyer, what does that make him? A lawyer too? That just doesn't work. He's not a lawyer, he would never be that. That's not him at all.'

At this time in the future the author would note that the brooch had quintupled in value and provenance in the imagination of his inquisitor and knew that he could not answer the questions asked of him. But when pinned to the side of a murky station sandwich outlet two years on, he would realise that the very last thing the person before him brandishing his book wanted was answers, different or otherwise.

There would be other questions about the piece of paper left lying on the road, the accident in the tunnel, the gold coins and the woman with ravens in her hair (was she the sister of the woman with pigtails on the course?). He would want to say that none of that mattered, as in the sequel they would all be killed when the Earth was destroyed by huge bullets of meteor and smaller fragments of Bruce Willis that crushed its surface, impacting at millions of miles an hour, but found that he couldn't.

'Why don't you answer our questions on the website?' this man would ask him, writing something down on a particularly large tab jutting out of his copy of the book about halfway through.

'What website?'

The man in the khaki trousers, standing on this station platform by the sandwich kiosk, would be aghast at this, and the author would take it as his chance to leave, fast – down some stairs that led to more platforms and away from the exit he needed to take.

'That's the problem,' his wife would say at regular intervals two years earlier. 'You cannot just hint at a past and future for these people and expect your readers to accept it. They need closure, or at least a degree of certainty about characters they have shared the chapters with.'

'So why don't *they* give them whatever is needed? Why does it have to come from me?' He could never get why people didn't get this.

She looked at him in the way others would; in the way his agent did when he first tried to explain that it was not that type of book.

'What type?'

'*That* type.'

His agent stood before him and made a kind of wheeling

motion with his arm. The author wondered how he knew that this meant, 'And the type *is*?' When sometimes the same motion would mean, 'Give me some more here,' or, 'Don't you see that is precisely what I mean?' But it had been an inquisition as to type, and the noncommittal shrug he chose from his own armoury of non-verbal gestures wasn't the answer the wheeling motion had required.

'You can't just do that. As a writer you have a responsibility to your audience. They expect you to be at least half of their imagination.'

'But that is it, you see. I won't be. This is exactly the type of book it is not. The people I write about will not all walk down from Waltons' Mountain and make pie together at the end of the story. I pass the responsibility for everything that happens to anyone who chooses to read it. They have to own it themselves.'

'They won't like it,' his agent had said.

'They won't like it,' his wife said.

'*We don't like it!*' the interrogator in khaki flares would scream after him down the steps two years later. '*Check the website, mate!*'

But he didn't mind. He had wanted to write about the two doors he believed people, those who chose to read his book, his agent, anyone, stood before. One was clearly marked 'Door A'. Behind it were all the usual consequences of choosing to go through. What? Confusion, unhappiness, anger, negativity. All that stuff.

The other was marked 'Door B'. Behind this door would be change, new openings, positivity; whatever they chose. Anyone could keep the images of these doors in their head. At any given time, before a decision, an argument, an impulse, they could make their choice of which door to walk through. Eventually, he hoped, their choices would lead them more regularly through 'Door B'. They would build this into a new, enlightened version of their instinct. Maybe he would write about this in another chapter. Maybe he had already written it somewhere but had forgotten where he put it.

All of these thoughts careered around his head as he stood there outside Green Park station looking at a space that a man in a baseball cap had occupied moments before.

He walked for a while, keeping the park on his left. What was this about instinct? He knew that when he sat down and planned a chapter he became consumed with the words, both the ones that came but were not right, and the right ones that lay behind that wouldn't come. At other times he sat and watched his fingers fly over the keyboard like a tightrope walker marvelling at his feet nurturing the rope that sliced in two the chasm beneath it. The words came at a rush and, when he read them back, he knew they only partly belonged to him.

At these times he was the greatest he could be. Then, when he really thought about this, he became a mere observer of greatness. An outsider looking in at what others could do. Yet still he found the connection hard to make.

As he looked at the trees tinged with orange and gold, feeling the fingers of autumn curl around his cheeks, he felt a moment of peace again. A true connection that offered him up to another life.

Was this the time the chapters could all come together? Would the man in the cap in the bar meet the poet? What of the ginger dreamer? What would be the link that wove through them like a thread, enabling them to see each other and themselves in clarity at last? Would the lawyer with the brooch and her former husband, who finally left the past behind to make a new life for himself, find a greater part of herself in the lists she made in a service area off the M4?

Did he have to decide and then tell everyone about it? Was his agent right?

'Offer them the kind of clues you write about. You know the three questions, the bloke with two shadows, that type of thing. Throw me a bone here.'

'But those are the clues, aren't they?'

'What?'

'The three questions, the accidental wisdom of the poet. Those are the clues.'

'OK, throw me some more.'

He had wanted to say that the signs people found when they are looking for them were not signs at all. It was the ones that crept up on them when they were distracted by their imagined wisdom that counted. However, he could picture the wheeling arm again. This time it said, 'Give me another chapter, one that ties up a few of the loose ends.'

'Can't you write another chapter?' his wife had asked helpfully. 'You know, one that ties up some of the loose ends.'

'You mean write an epilogue that tells everyone how it all worked out in five years?' He tried to put a snort into his voice.

'That would be nice,' she said. But he had stopped listening way before she had stopped talking. That wasn't it at all. It wasn't that he believed there were no happy endings, he just wanted others to construct them and own them for themselves.

'Why don't you write a chapter about you, the author, and all the things you have been thinking when you put this together?'

There was no question of that. He was not a character in this book. He did not want them knowing him and, as a result of that knowledge, place in context the things that should exist only in readers' imaginations, their futures.

He decided to walk and leave his direction to instinct. It had happened before. He had stood on the edge of a pavement and watched the two shadows that stretched away from his body separate him from all the one-shadowed beings bustling around. He had realised things that had no words of explanation and no place for meaning, but found himself in them in any event. At other times he had put this down to tiredness or alcohol induced malaise, but never been convinced by the explanation.

Now he walked, not looking for a thread that would please his agent and his wife, binding all this together. It was a bright October afternoon and he found himself following the shadows that played between the cracks in paving slabs on the path. He walked with Mayfair on his right and slipped through past Victoria to Pimlico, not recognising any part of the area. He may have driven this way before to avoid congestion or in search of a post office, but had no memory of doing so. He may have taken a taxi this way on the road to somewhere else, but this was not a part of his London, the part that led home.

He found a sense of wonder in the freedom of movement. His trainers felt soft and relenting against London's unforgiving pavements, his step light and easy. He had no bags with him and no time to keep. Even the hum of traffic fell in rhythm with his progress, and the further he walked the more at peace he became. It was a feeling of release, the baton change between conscious action and instinct. Was he really the designer? Could the perfection of this moment be an extension of his thoughts, or even the truth that lay behind them?

He walked for a time he couldn't put a number to and found himself at a place where he stopped, not just to avoid walking into the traffic that piled in each direction on the road before him. He felt the need to look around him. The road that stretched away from where he stood divided into a fork. The sun was very low, casting long shadows down the road leading off to the right, committing it to an early evening darkness. He checked his watch, it was just before five. The road that stretched away from it to the left was bathed in a glow that defied the night.

His experience called him left, but this was a journey of instinct. It took him down the narrow road to the right of the building. It was a lane cluttered with builders' debris and cars with broken spirits, scratched paintwork and bumper stickers that had once been amusing to someone following behind. He couldn't see where the road turned at the end but knew that was where he was heading. There was a clatter above him that may have been a window banging against its frame, and he looked up to check its source. He saw a caucus of crows circling the buildings, and one or two alight on precarious ladder fire escapes that clung to the walls. The motion of looking up automatically made him check his progress, enabling him to avoid an uneven dip in the path he was following. He couldn't see the source of the noise, but when he looked down again to watch where he was walking he saw a slip of paper lying in the road. It was folded and looked as if this had been recently and neatly done.

He picked it up and unfolded it. There were just four numbers written on the paper: 1, 1, 2, 0. He placed it in his pocket. He failed to see a piece of heavy material, as if torn from a jacket, hanging off a nail just behind him.

It was time to go home and write a chapter about the author.

The Beginning (Reprise)

'So that's what it is all about. I have to learn to trust the design. To understand I can have everything I want if I simply recognise who I truly am? Then I can go ahead and design it.'

'No.'

'No, which? What? No to which part?'

'Just no.'

'Hey, is this one of those clever word game things where you now say that the reverse of "no" is "on", and all I have to do is reverse no and I can turn it all on?'

'No.'

'Come on, work with me here. I know I have to look for the clues and that I can discover answers in the patterns they, you know, describe.'

'What book have you been reading? I do not recall any reference to describing patterns.'

'Well, I read between the lines. Isn't that what I was supposed to do? Discover the message, figure it out for myself, understand what it was telling me.'

'No.'

'No?'

'Listen to what you said. You said you have to learn to trust the design. You also asked if this was what you were supposed to do.'

'Oh, come on, those were just words.'

'Where do you suppose they came from?'

'My head; the part of my brain that turns electrical impulses into sounds and transmits them to my voice box.'

'What, and those words just sat there waiting as part of a big bang theory before exploding in a random way to form your conversation, did they? What are we witnessing now – haphazard and purposeless sounds hurtling away from a central vocal explosion, creating sense where the law of probability just gives up and allows it to happen?'

'No.'

'No, which? What? No to which part?'

'No, piss off and leave me alone.'

What if the words did not come from your brain, but from the universe? What if all there is adds up to a core of intelligence that acts as your tool, and does precisely as it is told by you? Then there would be nothing to learn, would there, and everything to do.'

'So I confuse this toolbox universe by saying I have to learn things; by saying that I am supposed to do things…'

The universe is not capable of confusion. It is pure intelligence. There can be no possibility of that happening. Just as there is no random, no chance.'

'And no coincidences? What about those times when we are thinking about someone and the next moment we receive a text from them. You are searching for the name of that tall bloke with hair and a beard in the movie about geese, and two people are talking about him on a train ten minutes later?'

What does your instinct say about that? If you listen to your instinct you will start to ask yourself different questions.'

'My instinct tells me that stuff just happens. In the same way that it doesn't happen sometimes, and because it doesn't happen we fail to spot the absence of it happening. We just recognise it when it happens. Coincidences don't happen all the time. I guess when they don't they're just called incidents.'

What if that is not your instincts, but just your humanity searching for words and explanations that fit your pre-existing boundaries? You seek a reason and settle for the one that fits into the way you know things to be. Then you use the vehicle of your language to transport it into reality. It is there you put your marker down and call it "truth" '

'And we get all of this wrong, and this universe watches over us and sniggers at our ineptitude?'

This would be the separate, out there, omni-place that exists above and beyond you, would it?'

'You tell me.'

No, tell yourself. Move beyond your boundaries. Stop listening to your language for a moment and tune into your instinct.'

'My instinct has been formed by my earthly experiences. I can't get beyond that.'

That is what the pre-existing explanation says, all you have just done is to use your language to call it truth.'

'I can't be condemned for that, can I?'

'By whom or what exactly?'

'I've got some pre-existing explanation that is using the vehicle of my language to transport the answer to that into reality here. Help!'

'Can I tell you a story?'

'Will it help?'

'It will, if you listen to it with your instinct and don't attempt to encircle it with explanations that work for you in the context of your life here.'

'Tell me the story.'

'A woman comes home from her place of work. She has a highly important job that involves a great deal of technical know-how and understanding. She removes her coat, carries her briefcase into the main living area… What would your pre-programmed vehicle of language call that? A "sitting room" or "lounge", maybe? Once there, she takes some papers out of her case which she wants to work on prior to a very important meeting the next day. The woman leaves these papers on a table in the room.

'There is a lot of paperwork, much of it marked confidential and highly sensitive. It contains graphs, financial statements, data projections and implementation plans, studded with the occasional pie diagram and multicoloured bar chart, replete with margin notes and annotations.

'She goes into her kitchen to make herself a drink, before facing her young family, who have been eagerly awaiting her return from work and who are, at that time, being towelled down and readied for their time together.

'Her two young children are aged two and four. They are curious, bright and naturally lively by nature. They are explorers, too young yet to recognise that this is what they will always be. However, they do not see their exploration as a game. To them their world is fascinating, still new, and their job is to run around in it seeking answers among the fun.

'As the woman stands in her kitchen waiting for the kettle to boil she hears conversation coming from the next room, the one in which she has left the papers on the table. She pokes her head out of the kitchen doorway and sees her two children. The eldest one has moved a chair to enable her to clamber up to table height. The younger one is sitting on the chair beside his sister. They have taken some of their mother's papers from the pile and are examining them together. The children are not damaging the papers in any

way; in fact she is amazed to watch the deference with which they treat them.

"'What's that?" the little boy asks his sister, pointing at a page adorned with a bar chart wallpapered with numbers and notes.*

"'Those are the houses where tall people live," replies his sister. "And those are the shopping lists of the things they need to buy," she adds, indicating the lists of calculus spreading out across the next two pages. Her conviction and sagacity appears to grow the more her brother nods his approval and acceptance of this meted wisdom.*

'As the woman watches, the little girl answers all of her brother's questions, carefully and sincerely. Sometimes she ponders for a while before giving her reply, but she always offers full explanations to the questions asked of her.*

'The silhouette of the mother softens against the kitchen door jamb. As she stands apart from them witnessing their youthful reconnaissance she realises she has a series of choices. She can walk into the room and exchange the papers for some of her children's books containing stories they know, illustrated with images they will easily understand.*

'She could spend time deciphering the documents for her children, dumbing down the concepts but still using terms galaxies away from their experience and ability to grasp.'*

'Or?'

'Or?'

'Or she can accept the situation as being perfect. She can allow her children to guess and seek and explore, knowing that they have no language to understand and no need for it.'

'The only word you missed was "yet". They have no need for understanding yet. The mother cannot imagine two and four-year-olds with a full take on market forecasts and budgetary analysis. She knows that the moments of not knowing make the moments of knowing timely, wonderful. She doesn't judge her children for not understanding. She just loves them. If they don't have the words they will find ones that appear to fit. They are explorers. That is what they do.'*

'What if they find wrong interpretations of the things in front of them? What if their version of the answers can cause damage, not only to them but others around them?'

'What if the uncommonality of language moves in two directions? What if, where the answers are, there is no meaning for words such as "wrong"* and "damage"? *What if this is the greatest thing the children can discover amidst the oceans, and planets, and protons, and dreams? You mentioned perfection before. A realisation of this is to knock on the door of where perfect resides. If there is no "bar chart" in the vocabulary of the children, they must see them as houses where tall people live. It makes perfect sense. They can even prove that these are houses by comparing them with pictures of tall houses they have seen. They could even wave these pictures at other people and use their language to convince them, too.'*

'In your story, who is the mother?'

'She lives in the houses with the tall people.'

'So I am a child? I am not able to grasp who the mother is?'

'There it is again – the missing word "yet". You asked the question, so you must presume that there is still something you need to learn. That the information is outside of you.'

'Go on, imagine this is something I can experience by hearing about it from you.'

'The mother is as much a part of the children as the children are of her. In her love for them and theirs for her, there is no place where she is separate from them. They are the same.'

'Do the children feel separate from her?'

'In the place where the tall people live they may experience separation that has no reality, but it feels as real as the walls of the houses.'

'Jeez, this is so hard! You can get all of this so wrong, can't you?'

'And there it is.'

'It is?'

'Oh yes. You arrive at the centre by feeling your way around the walls on the perimeter with your eyes closed. At the centre there is for you, all of you, the sense that everything is a test; an exercise, maybe. Scientists may call it an experiment, academics an exam, sportsmen a competition, Chinese philosophers the active male and female principles of the universe, lawyers a trial.

You have made it the central tenet around which everything else pivots. You could be right, or wrong. Something could be good, but it could be bad. On this basis you judge yourself and those others around you.'

'Just like the kids were wrong about the tall houses?'

'Were they?'

'Well, they were wrong, weren't they? It was a bar chart. It wasn't the profiled outline of a town or street.'

'What are you going to do now? Wave around pictures at me as evidence? Prove it to me? Make me wrong so you can be right? What if I were to respond by taking you to a place where there could be no right and no wrong? No tests, nothing to fail and no cases to lose. No yin and no yang.'

'It would – I don't know. It would…'

'Having problems with the words you would like to use to describe how that would feel? Why not just make some up?'

'You can't just make words up. It is too stressful.'

'Really? You have before. Where do you think the word "stress" comes from? There was a word the modern world had urgent need of. And up it pops into your language. Let us see, there is the French estresse, meaning narrowness or constricting, and the Latin strictus. Roll it all up, make it into a new word and put that in a box.'

'You are telling me that there are no tests; nothing we need get right or wrong; nothing we have to achieve?'

'How does that feel?'

'It just doesn't compute.'

'In the same way that you cannot recall the last time you felt gudzuntick?'

'What's that?'

'It has no meaning. I just made it up. You cannot feel it because it does not have any meaning within your vocabulary.'

'OK, I think my brain is about to explode here. I'm allowed that one because it derives, by the way, from the Latin ex meaning out, and plaudere to clap.'

'That is good, and very close. Now you can try the Latin word expereriri, because down a short but tortuous linguistic path it leads to the word experience. Why not just go crazy and experience things for a while? Forget judging them, forget wondering if they are right or good or useful.

'What would it take for you to experience with your instincts and to trust them?'

'It would be like starting anew. I almost said, "learning to start anew" then; you know, using the "l" word.'

'But you did not say that.'

'No.'

'Why not?'

'To be honest, I think it made me feel a little gudzuntick.'

'*I see.*'

'Trusting is the hardest thing, though. Can you give me a hand with that?'

'*Look both inside and outside of yourself for the clues from the universe. Let your instinct recognise and follow them and the trust will come. But in the meantime I would take something for that gudzuntick.*'

The Beginning

Look for your clues.
Just because they are not obvious,
or easy to find, doesn't mean that they are not there.
If you are part of the sending, projecting and
planting, then who knows yourself better?

Happy hunting.

Lightning Source UK Ltd.
Milton Keynes UK
15 July 2010

157063UK00001B/7/P